THE RIGHT TO KNOW

JAMES MADISON. PRESIDENT OF THE USA,
1822.
'A popular government, without popular information
or the means of acquiring it, is but a prologue to a
farce or a tragedy; or, perhaps both. Knowledge will
forever govern ignorance; and a people who mean to
be their own governors must arm themselves with the
power which knowledge gives.'

MICHAEL HESELTINE, SECRETARY OF STATE
FOR DEFENCE, NOVEMBER 1984
'One of the things which influenced my mind
profoundly when I came to the original judgement on
how to deal with the 'Crown Jewels' was that it was
quite apparent to me that the more information we
provided the more it would be argued yet more
information was needed.'

The Right To Know
The Inside Story of the *Belgrano* Affair
CLIVE PONTING

SPHERE BOOKS LIMITED
London and Sydney

First published in Great Britain by
Sphere Books Ltd 1985
30–32 Gray's Inn Road, London WC1X 8JL
Copyright © 1985 by Clive Ponting

Publisher's Note
All the material in this book is drawn from publicly
available information including the proceedings
at Clive Ponting's Old Bailey trial.

TRADE
MARK

Set in Plantin

Printed and bound in Great Britain by
Cox & Wyman Ltd, Reading

To Sally

CONTENTS

PREFACE

This book is about official secrecy, its history, the circumstances that led up to my own trial at the Old Bailey and the future of the official secrecy and the debate about freedom of information. Much of the book is based on my own researches into the subject in the process of developing my defence at the Old Bailey trial. But no book, let alone the work involved in preparing for a major trial, is a solo effort and this book and the defence case at the trial would have been impossible without the help of many others.

My solicitor, Brian Raymond, was a tower of strength throughout and he went far beyond the call of duty in the effort he devoted to the case. He was not just a solicitor but a close friend. My QC, Bruce Laughland, and junior counsel, Jonathan Caplan, similarly threw themselves wholeheartedly into the case and displayed their great skill tellingly in the court. It was a privilege to work with such a dedicated legal team. From the media David Leigh, of the *Observer*, offered help when it was most needed and has been a great friend from the start. Similarly, Duncan Campbell, of the *New Statesman*, offered help at the beginning and continued to do so throughout. Richard Norton-Taylor, of the *Guardian*, was tireless in his efforts, and Peter Hennessy gave constant encouragement. Outside the media John Ward, General Secretary of the FDA, gave unstinting help in difficult circumstances and Des Wilson and James Michael of the Freedom of Information Campaign and Larry Gostin, Marie Staunton and Barbara Cohen of NCCL provided major support. I also received enormous encouragement from friends who are still in the Ministry of Defence. For obvious reasons I cannot name them but they know who they are and how much they helped.

Most of all I have to thank my wife, Sally, who lived through it all and shared the highs and the lows, and gave me constant support through the most difficult period of our lives.

INTRODUCTION

On 28 January 1985 I stood in the dock of No. 2 Court at the Old Bailey charged under Section 2 of the Official Secrets Act. I was accused of disclosing 'official information' without authority to an unauthorised person. The 'official information' was two documents about events in the South Atlantic and the sinking of the Argentinian cruiser *General Belgrano* in May 1982. The Government had already admitted, during the committal proceedings at Bow Street Magistrates Court, that national security was not involved. The documents had been sent to a Member of Parliament and passed to a Select Committee of the House of Commons where they had played an essential part in its enquiries into the sinking.

I found it difficult to believe this could be happening to me. Many others were equally incredulous and outraged that this trial should be taking place. There had been calls from the leader of the Labour party, Neil Kinnock, the Liberal Party, and the leader of the SDP, David Owen, for the prosecution to be dropped. Media interest in the trial was intense and many commentators had said that the trial would be the biggest test of the Official Secrets Acts in their hundred-year history. Channel 4 planned to show a thirty-minute reconstruction of the day's events every night.

A number of questions remained unresolved. Why did Parliament not have the right to know this information? Why had the old, discredited Official Secrets Acts been wheeled out yet again when national security was not involved and the only matter at risk was the political reputation of certain Government Ministers? Why were events in the South Atlantic nearly three years before the trial still a live issue?

Why was the Foreign Affairs committee of the House of Commons conducting a major enquiry?

Before the trial there had been much debate about the role and duties of civil servants. Were they just the blind servants of Ministers doing only what they were told or could there be circumstances when they might have a higher loyalty either to Parliament or possibly to the public interest? Since my arrest there has been a major debate inside the Civil Service, and in particular my own trade union, the First Division Association, about the role of the Civil Service. By the end of 1984 the FDA had produced a draft Code of Ethics designed to deal with some of the dilemmas that could face civil servants. The more difficult question was whether Ministers would accept such a Code.

My case had also raised questions about the style of the Thatcher Government, its relationship with Parliament, the way in which it handled the flow of information and whether it was too authoritarian. Did the Government expect civil servants simply to carry out unhesitatingly Ministerial policies, and did the Government with its large majority in the House of Commons believe that it had the power to act without consensus and in opposition to the view of large sections of the country?

The case had also raised vitally important legal issues, and not just about the use of the discredited Section 2. My defence would be that I had acted 'in the interests of the State'. But just what was the 'State' in English law and what were its 'interests'? Could this be left to the jury to decide at the end of the trial once they had heard all the evidence, or would the prosecution try to use the argument that 'the interests of the State' had to be defined by the Government of the day? If the latter definition was correct then 'the interests of the State' would be the same as 'the political interests of the Government'. This would be a radical new departure in English law that would have profound implications and could, many people had argued, be the first step on the road to greater authoritarianism. Would the judge take the classic position of protecting the wider public interest from the power of the Government or would he back the Government?

A major political row about the conduct of the trial had broken out only a week before it was due to start. At the last moment the Secretary of State for Defence, Michael Heseltine, had agreed to introduce into the trial a 'Top Secret' Ministry of Defence study of the sinking of the *Belgrano* that I had written and which had become known as the 'Crown Jewels'. Only six copies had been made. Now it was to be given to the twelve jurors, all the lawyers and barristers involved and it would be heard by all the court officials. Clearly the Government were playing for high stakes in their attempt to convict me. When it was decided that the document should be introduced, the jury had to be vetted – in a trial where the prosecution had already admitted that national security was not involved in any way. Parts of the trial would also have to be held *in camera*. David Steel, the Liberal leader, said that the forthcoming trial would be 'an East-European style secret trial' and Roy Hattersley, Deputy Leader of the Labour party, had earlier described it as a 'show trial'.

It has always been the conventional view that there are no political trials in Britain. But my own trial was clearly going to be the most 'political' trial this century. The essence of my defence was that Ministers had misled Parliament. The prosecution, after an initial reluctance, seemed willing to fight us on this ground. Their case would be that the decisions taken in April and May 1982 had been correct, that it was right to sink the *Belgrano* and that Ministers had subsequently acted perfectly reasonably. In the trial these positions would be argued out in public. The battlefield would be internal MOD documents, some of them only six or seven months old, and they would be revealed for the public to gaze at the internal and high-level workings of a Government department. A great deal was at stake in the trial – not just my liberty.

The immediate chain of events leading to my trial at the Old Bailey began in July 1984. I sent two documents to Tam Dalyell who passed them to Sir Anthony Kershaw, the chairman of the Select Committee that was being misled by the Government. Kershaw handed them to Michael Heseltine, the Secretary of State for Defence, who promptly called in the Ministry of Defence police to investigate the 'leak'. Within two days of the investigation starting I signed a statement admitting that I had sent the papers to Dalyell and explaining why I had taken that decision. After discussions with senior civil servants in MOD I felt sure that they had assured me that there was no question of a prosecution under the Official Secrets Act and that my resignation would be 'the end of the matter'. I resigned from the Civil Service. Four days later I was told that Ministers wanted a prosecution, against the advice of the police and the Civil Service, and that the papers were being sent to the Director of Public Prosecutions. The day after they arrived, after consultations with the Attorney-General for about ten minutes at the end of a phone (he was on holiday in France) I was arrested and charged. Suddenly I found myself appearing at Bow Street Magistrates Court, surrounded by the media and escaping from the court in a police van to avoid the photographers. It was a very different world from the Civil Service.

I had joined the Civil Service in 1970 as an Assistant Principal – the conventional way for a budding mandarin to start his career. I was not an idealist, but I did have hopes that this was to be a job where rational decision taking and analysis of problems would help, at least in a small way, to provide good government. By 1984 I had become increasingly disenchanted with the Civil Service and work in the Ministry of Defence for three reasons.

First, I had found that the Civil Service itself was introverted, complacent and unable to take decisions or manage either its staff or the many operations it controlled. The world of the top civil servant revolves around relations with Ministers and high-level policy discussions. Few civil servants have any experience of the world outside Whitehall or indeed outside their own departments. There are virtually no exchanges with industry or the rest of the public sector and even jobs in the Cabinet office or other central departments are rare. This gives a very distorted perspective where 'the interests of the department' come at the top of the list of priorities. Loyalty to the department is the greatest virtue for a civil servant. This concentration on high-level policy-making is at the expense of the management of the complex functions that Government controls. Jobs involving management rather than policy-making are held in low esteem by top civil servants. The result is that the best people do not want to work in such jobs and so the level of performance in these areas is correspondingly low. Inefficiency and waste is endemic and little effort is devoted to removing it.

The style favoured by top civil servants is bland and neutral. Toughness, the ability to take decisions and carry through difficult policies are not considered to be great virtues. Problems are not there to be solved but avoided, and the greatest of all abilities is to be able to 'draft round' a problem.

The second reason for my growing disenchantment with the world of Whitehall was that life with Ministers was becoming increasingly difficult. The new Tory administration elected in 1979 made it clear that they appeared to despise the Civil Service and although I shared their belief that much could be done to improve Whitehall, the way in which Ministers went about the task only lowered morale. Cuts in staff numbers were imposed without any consideration of what they would entail in terms of workload or service to the public. Pay agreements were torn up without consultation. But more important it was made clear that the Civil Service was too devoted to 'consensus politics' and not the new school of 'commitment politics'. The only function of a non-political Civil Service must be to provide independent analysis and rational argument as the basis on which Ministers can take decisions which the Civil Service then carry out. Increasingly from 1979 Ministers made it clear that they knew what solutions they wanted and the role of the Civil Service was to implement policies without argument. At the top of the Civil Service a greater degree of political commitment to the policies of the Government was expected. Top mandarins in the Treasury were expected to be monetarists. Loyalty and not the ability to produce well-reasoned argument was to be the chief characteristic of the new breed of top civil servants. The Prime Minister took a close personal interest in appointments at the top and carefully selected the right men who had the right attitudes. This was politicisation of the Civil Service via the back door.

The third factor was that fifteen years' hard work battling with the wasteful military bureaucracy had been a disillusioning experience. Each of the three Services is a very strong pressure group lobbying to preserve its vested interests. Rational argument is almost impossible and most civil servants can only survive in the Ministry of Defence by not fighting the Services and allowing them to continue with their gold-plated schemes and projects and their generally luxurious style of life. Every privilege and obscure part of the organisation is defended with equal tenacity from the number of mess waiters and gardeners at tiny training establishments to high cost and wasteful equipment projects with over-complex specifications. All of that is a different story and not one that I can safely tell whilst Section 2 of the Official Secrets Act remains on the statute book. However, I can outline my career as the background to events that led to my arrest and trial.

I was born in April 1946, part of the post-war baby boom. I was brought up in a quiet middle class suburb of Bristol, an only child. From the local primary school I gained a scholarship in the '11 plus' to the main local grammar school – Bristol Grammar School. This was a direct-grant school which imitated many of the customs of the well-known public schools and had a high reputation for academic achievement. It was always assumed at school that anybody who got reasonable 'A' level results would go on to University and when in 1965 I passed 3 'A' levels, in History, Geography and Economics, I followed the usual path. I went to Reading University to read History. In my last year when I was starting to think about possible careers, I went along to a talk by somebody from the Civil Service Commission. Despite his glowing descriptions of the wonderful jobs on offer, I decided against the Civil Service because it was probably full of people from Oxbridge. I was right – it is. Instead, after finals, I decided to have a go at research for a PhD, working through the archives at the dirty, overcrowded rooms of the Public Record Office in Chancery Lane. The more I read the more I became interested in public administration.

After the usual set of tests lasting for two days at the Civil Service Selection Board and a final interview I joined the Ministry of Technology in August 1970 only to find it was being broken up by the newly elected Heath Government. I passed rapidly through the Ministry of Aviation Supply and finally into Defence. The career of a trainee mandarin follows a basic pattern of 'on the job' training and a rapid change of jobs every six or nine months with a spell at the Civil Service College. Then I had a spell as Private Secretary to one of the Permanent Secretaries in MOD, Sir Michael Cary (the son of the novelist Joyce Cary).

My first proper job came as a Principal, the 'desk-level' in the administrative Civil Service when you are expected to become the 'expert' on a detailed area of policy. I was dealing with shipbuilding policy. My immediate boss was Clive Whitmore, later to be Private Secretary to Mrs Thatcher and by 1983 Permanent Secretary in MOD. Then my next two and a half years were spent controlling the equipment programme for the Army – £1 billion a year budget.   .

Just after the 1979 election I had a new job working for Sir Derek Rayner, who had been brought in from Marks & Spencer to cut out waste in the Civil Service and improve efficiency in Whitehall. Each department in Whitehall had to provide a Principal to work full-time with Sir Derek in investigating one area of operations and the results had to be presented in a report direct to a Minister and Sir Derek within sixty days. I studied the supply of food to the Armed Forces, an area that had supposedly been 'rationalised' and made highly efficient in the late 1960s. Instead I found massive inefficiency everywhere – huge stocks of food far in excess of requirements, little or no co-ordination between the three Services and an almost complete lack of accounts that would enable people to find out what everything costed and measure the efficiency of the whole operation. Worse still nobody seemed to care whether or not the system was operating efficiently – provided it produced the goods at the right time. At the end of the study I wrote a report recommending savings of about £12 million in food stocks, about £1–3 million a year through economies in the running of the supply system and the creation of a single integrated system run by someone who would actually be accountable for the cost effective management of resources.

Once all the studies were complete Sir Derek Rayner held a conference at the Civil Service College – an old country house in delightful grounds – at Sunningdale. Every department had found areas of waste. It was a sobering experience, that showed me how deeply ingrained was the habit of Whitehall inefficiency. The Cabinet were to discuss a report from Sir Derek early in October 1979 and he asked me, together with my colleague from the Department of Health and Social Security, to go along with him to brief Mrs Thatcher for the meeting. One afternoon we went over to No. 10 and sitting in the Prime Minister's office on the first floor we told our stories about our investigations. Mrs Thatcher was very enthusiastic; we were confirming all her instinctive beliefs about how Whitehall really operated. To my amazement at the end of the meeting, the Prime Minister suddenly decided that we should accompany Sir Derek when he went to brief the Cabinet. This was an unprecedented decision. Mere Principals did not go to the Cabinet! But the Secretary of the Cabinet, Sir John Hunt, did not bat an eyelid and took us downstairs to show us where we would be sitting in the Cabinet Room.

There was a hurried round of activity as I had to see Francis Pym, the Secretary of State for Defence, and brief him on what I was going to say to his colleagues about the efficiency (or lack of it) in MOD. But he was very relaxed and the next day even joined in the gales of laughter that greeted our choicest selection of anecdotes about the real Whitehall.

They were received so enthusiastically I felt sure this would be the start of some real changes. I was, however, underestimating the ability of the bureaucracy in Whitehall to avoid fundamental reforms. My report was simply never implemented. After three years of further work, carried out this time by those involved in running the existing system and therefore with a vested interest in maintaining the status quo, it was agreed that there should be no radical changes and that the old ways of working should continue. I learnt that even with the support of the Prime Minister changing Whitehall is far from easy, and in many cases impossible. There was at least one surprising result from this episode – one day in the spring of 1980 a letter from No. 10 arrived saying that my name was to go forward for an OBE in the Birthday Honours in June 1980.

After my abortive attempts to save about £15 million I was posted to the division responsible for planning the £12 billion a year Defence programme and negotiating with the Treasury in the annual round of public expenditure planning. This was a time of frantic effort and hurried decisions. Within the space of twelve months we held two reviews of Defence spending, introduced a moratorium in an attempt to keep expenditure within the cash limit agreed with the Treasury and early in 1981 we had to redesign the whole system of financial planning within the Ministry.

In September 1981 I was promoted to Assistant Secretary at the age of thirty-five. As a typical head of a division in MOD HQ I was responsible for about twenty-five or thirty people, with a room of my own (for the first time) and, most important in terms of status, my own secretary! This is the level at which there is a real interface between higher level policy-making, dealing direct with Ministers, and the execution of policy. I was put in charge of a division that dealt with two areas of work. The first was training in the Services and I embarked on a series of studies that were to take me round various obscure parts of the Armed Forces. But the most bizarre task was to look into why the Services employed about 175 servicemen to sit in laboratories all day and make false teeth for other servicemen at twice the price of the commercial laboratories that supplied the whole of the National Health Service. Progress in all these studies was slow, the battles exhausting, but in the end some small victories for efficiency and rationality were achieved. The other part of my division dealt with legal questions. In the time-honoured tradition of the Civil Service cult of the amateur I did not have a single lawyer dealing with the subject. In 1982 we were suddenly plunged into the Falklands crisis and I had to become an instant expert on the Geneva Convention, treatment of prisoners of war, the requisitioning of merchant ships and a hundred and one other problems thrown up by the campaign. Hardly any of us had been involved in fighting a war before and we all had to learn as we went along.

Another area of great interest was prosecutions under the Official Secrets Acts! Many cases passed through my office on the way to the Director of Public Prosecutions and the Attorney-General. It was my job to study the terms of the Acts, advising the Secretary of State on the political and publicity aspects of cases, though not the prosecution of Sarah Tisdall, as has been alleged. That case was handled by the Metropolitan Police. It did not cross my mind that I too would become a 'case' to be dealt with in the same way and that I would spend six months of my life thinking of little else but the Official Secrets Acts and preparing for my own trial at the Old Bailey. The peculiar series of events that led to my trial came about only after I moved to my second job as an Assistant Secretary – Head of Defence Secretariat 5 in March 1984. It was here that I came up against circumstances I had never seen before in my career and faced the most difficult decision of my life.

The decision I took and its consequences are the subject of the second part of this book. But it is impossible to understand why things happened as they did without investigating official secrecy and its domination of life inside Whitehall. The first two chapters therefore deal with the history and operations of the Official Secrets Acts and why reform has been blocked by Whitehall.

PART I
OFFICIAL SECRECY

CHAPTER ONE

THE OFFICIAL SECRETS ACTS AND WHITEHALL SECRECY

The centenary of the Official Secrets Acts is rapidly approaching. The first Act became law in 1889: it was radically revised and extended in 1911 and further amended in 1920. There has been only one reduction in the scope of the Acts: in 1939 after a major political row involving the attempted use of the Acts against a Member of Parliament. I am sure that everybody in this country would accept the need for criminal sanctions against those who deliberately betray the nation's secrets to a foreign power whether for ideological or financial reasons. Severe powers against such action are contained in Section 1 of the 1911 Act and have only rarely been used in a controversial way. What has caused persistent controversy has been the widespread use of the powers contained in Section 2 to prosecute individuals for releasing official information not involving national security, or to foreign powers or for financial gain.

Until 1888 there was no statute dealing with the protection of official information. It was the growing number of 'leaks' to the press in the middle of the nineteenth century that persuaded Lord Salisbury's Government that legislation was required. In the mid 19th century, the functions of government were extremely limited and most of the 'leaks' involved information about foreign affairs and diplomatic negotiations.

One of the first scandals involved the Colonial Office in November 1858. Two despatches revealing Government duplicity in the administration of the Ionian Islands were stolen by a William Guernsey and published in the *Daily News*. Guernsey was charged with larceny and prosecuted by the Attorney-General. He was well defended and the judge commended the action of the *Daily News* in publishing the despatches even though they were marked 'confidential'. The jury was out for only fifteen minutes and acquitted Guernsey.

However 'leaks' continued and in 1873, 1875 and 1884 circulars were issued by the Treasury threatening dismissal for any civil servant who deliberately disclosed official information. One of the most serious incidents occurred in 1878. Just before the Congress of Berlin, called to deal with the revolt in the Balkans, secret discussions between Britain and Russia on a joint approach to the Conference were published in *The Globe* before the Congress had opened. A clerk in the Foreign Office, Charles Marvin (who was also a correspondent for *The Globe* and endowed with a photographic memory), had memorised the text of the agreement and later copied it out in the office of the newspaper. There was fairly strong evidence that he had been paid by *The Globe* for this scoop. The problem was the nature of the charge to be made against Marvin. There was no doubt that he had communicated the information but that in itself was not an offence. He was eventually charged with larceny for stealing the paper on which he had written out the despatch. The evidence was thin and after three appearances at Bow Street the case was eventually dismissed.

Two further cases of 'leaks' in 1887 convinced the Government that legislation would have to be introduced. The first Bill to create a criminal offence was introduced in 1888 and called, interestingly, the 'Breach of Official Trust Bill'. Even at this early stage there was criticism from MPs that it might restrict access to information about corruption and malpractice in Government departments. Some MPs felt that the use of the criminal law should be restricted to the protection of national secrets. As a result the Bill was amended to allow a public interest defence.

The 1889 Act set the framework for all subsequent legislation. Section 1 dealt with spying. Section 2 dealt with the wider protection of official information. The relevant part of that section was:

Where a person, after having been entrusted in confidence by some officer under her Majesty the Queen with any document, sketch, plan, model, or information relating to any such place as aforesaid, or to the naval or military affairs of Her Majesty, wilfully and in breach of such confidence communicates the same when, in the interests of the State, it ought not to be communicated; he shall be guilty of a misdemeanour, and on conviction be liable to imprisonment, with or without hard labour, for a term not exceeding one year, or to a fine, or to both imprisonment and a fine.

This established the principle that the communication of official information by a person in a position of public trust was, in certain circumstances, subject to the criminal law. But, importantly, it limited the criminal law to those breaches which could be shown to be against the public interest.

A number of prosecutions under the 1889 Act were brought in the following years, but almost entirely under Section 1. As early as 1896 the Government introduced an amending Bill to shift the burden of proof from the prosecution onto the defence in certain circumstances, but it was eventually withdrawn. At intervals throughout the first decade of the 20th century the Government considered introducing proposals to tighten up the law. In March 1908 the Liberal Government introduced an amending Bill in the House of Lords. The press reacted sharply, fearing censorship from the new clause banning publication of certain official information and the Bill was withdrawn.

The 1909 'Plot'

Rather than abandon its proposals the Government merely waited for a more propitious occasion to re-introduce them. On 25 March 1909 the Prime Minister, Asquith, set up, at the request of the military, a sub-committee of the Committee of Imperial Defence on 'the nature and extent of the foreign espionage that is at present taking place in this country to consider whether there should be a system for co-ordinating

the monitoring of the movements of aliens and whether it is
desirable to increase the powers that we now possess of
dealing in times of emergency with persons suspected of
being spies or secret service agents'.

The Committee considered a number of papers all
concerned with espionage and the activities of spies and
foreigners. The paper from the Home Office on the 1889
Official Secrets Act only suggested amendments to Section 1
on spying and the Commissioner of Police made similar
suggestions. As the Secretary of the Committee wrote, an
amending Bill on these lines 'need contain no reference to the
publication of documents or information ... it would
therefore not be so controversial a nature or excite such
opposition as would be caused by any clause which might be
suspect of interfering with the liberties of the press' (as in the
1908 Bill). But at the third meeting of the Committee on 12
July 1909 Robert McKenna (First Lord of the Admiralty)
introduced a new thought:

> Mr McKenna pointed out that the *Daily Mail* had
> recently published details regarding one of our battle-
> ships which the Admiralty desired to keep secret. We
> ought to be in a position to prosecute the proprietor of
> the paper for doing this. We are, however, quite
> powerless in the matter, as the Official Secrets Act does
> not provide us with any machinery for instituting such a
> prosecution. If we knew the person who had com-
> municated the information to the paper we could
> prosecute that person under the Act, but in order to
> prove him guilty it would be necessary to vouch for the
> truth of the information that he had caused to be
> published. The actual publisher of the newspaper could
> not be touched.

The Committee reported on 24 July 1909 and recommended setting up a Secret Service Bureau. This was so
sensitive that only one copy of the proposals had been made.
On the Official Secrets Act itself, the Committee recommended that the proposals to amend Section 1 should be

introduced but that a separate Bill with the proposals from McKenna should be put forward after negotiations with the Press. The record of the Committee's thinking is absolutely frank about motive and tactics:

> They (the members of the Committee) are of the opinion that such a Bill would excite less opposition if it were introduced by the Secretary of State for War than by the Home Office, and that this might be done on the plea of its being a measure of precaution of great importance to national defence.

The Passing of the 1911 Act

In 1911 the Government was to follow this advice to the letter and the Bills were amalgamated in a single Official Secrets Act. Although debated in haste, the Act was not in fact drafted in haste; on the contrary, it had been carefully prepared and its extensive scope was well known to the Government. The Government also accepted the advice to wait for a suitable opportunity to introduce the Act so they could claim an urgent necessity based on national security and secure their aims with as little debate as possible. The opportunity came in the summer of 1911. There was an international crisis over Agadir in Morocco and war between Britain and Germany seemed close. The new Official Secrets Bill was introduced in the House of Lords and debated on 25 July. It repealed the 1889 Act and introduced a more draconian Section 1 and an all-embracing Section 2 covering both the communication and receipt of official information. *But Section 2 was not once mentioned during the parliamentary debates.* Haldane, introducing the Bill in the Lords, emphasised espionage and the careful consideration that had been given to the proposals, including placing the burden of proof on the defendant in the proposed Section 1. After just three other speeches the Bill was given a second reading.

The Bill's passage through the House of Commons was even more rapid. In just forty minutes late on the very hot summer morning of 18 August, long after Parliament normally rose for the recess, the Bill went through all the procedural stages – second reading, committee, and third reading. The crucial assurance was given by the Under-Secretary of State for War, Colonel Seely:

> It is undoubtedly in the public interest that this Bill should be passed, and passed at once. It is highly undesirable, no doubt, that any Bill should go through its stages so rapidly as this has done, and it certainly cannot be taken as a precedent. If my hon. Friends will read the Bill they will see that . . . the actual change in the law is slight, and it is perfectly true to say that none of His Majesty's loyal subjects run the least risk whatever of having their liberties infringed in any degree or particular whatever.

As we have seen the key change in the law was far from being 'slight' and the Government had never intended that it should be on a limited scale. The plot first proposed in 1909 was being implemented. The Attorney-General went even further in playing down the significance of the proposals:

> Of course, this House knows that the principle of this Bill is not new . . . There is nothing novel in the principle of the Bill.

The House immediately went into Committee and without discussion the Bill moved to its final stage without amendment. Only ten Labour members voted against. After a brief protest about the wording of Section 1 and a reference to Magna Carta the Bill was read a third time and completed all its Parliamentary procedures. *There had been no discussion at all of Section 2.*

The 1920 Act

Before considering the provisions of Section 2 as introduced in 1911 we need to look briefly at the 1920 Act which amended it. During the First World War a number of Defence of the Realm regulations had been made and when they lapsed at the end of the war the Government decided to set up an inter-departmental committee with representatives of the Admiralty, War Office and the Home Office. It was this committee that drafted the 1920 Bill, which had only a minor effect on the existing Section 2. Most of its provisions dealt with Section 1 – further easing the burden of proof on the prosecution and introducing new offences such as falsely pretending to be a person holding office under the Crown in order to gain entry to a prohibited place and interfering with the police or members of the armed forces in the vicinity of a prohibited place. It also contained a extraordinary new Section 7 making it a criminal offence to do any act preparatory to an offence under the Official Secrets Acts!

The Bill was introduced, again as in 1911, in the House of Lords in June 1920. In both Houses it had a much rougher passage than the 1911 Act. The Government, as before, argued that the Act was about espionage and that it made no new departures in the law. Nevertheless there was a considerable disquiet. Lord Parmoor, a Lord of Appeal, opposed the Bill 'because it will seriously interfere with ordinary freedom in various directions'. During the second reading debate in the Commons on 2 December 1920 there was considerable opposition to the new measure. The Attorney-General (Sir Gordon Hewart) continually implied that the Bill was concerned with spying and the improvements in the legislation against spying required by experience in the war and denied that it had anything to do with journalists or the press. The Government tactics were successful in that most of the debate was again concentrated on Section 1 rather than Section 2. But strong feelings were aroused, as one of the main opponents, the Liberal Sir Donald Maclean, said:

> I find it difficult to confine my language in regard to this Bill within the range of Parliamentary propriety. It is another attempt to clamp the powers of war on the liberties of the citizen in peace.

At one stage the Attorney-General grossly misled the Commons about the scope of the Bill when he claimed:

> We are dealing only with offences or suspected offences

under the principal Act (1911) of this Act. In other words, to put it shortly, we are dealing with spying and attempts at spying.

It is not clear how the Government's chief legal adviser could have come to such a conclusion.

What is Section 2?

The major features of the Official Secrets Acts were now established. As David Williams says in his book *Not in the Public Interest*:

> Such, then, is the present-day law on official secrets. It is all based on an ill-considered principal Act (1911) as amended by an over-simplified subsequent statute (1920). The first was enacted at the onset and the second during the aftermath of a spy-scare. Each was undoubtedly either inspired or endorsed by the War Office and the Admiralty. Together they have become one of the most ubiquitous, far-reaching and all-purpose blocks of statute law ever perpetrated in this country.

What does Section 2 of the Official Secrets Acts actually say? The amended text of the section is:-

> 2. Wrongful communication, etc, of information
> (1) If any person having in his possession or control (any secret official code word, or pass word, or) any sketch, plan, model, article, note, document, or information which relates to or is used in a prohibited place or anything in such a place, or which has been made or obtained in contravention of this Act, or which has been entrusted in confidence to him by any person holding office under His Majesty or which he has obtained [or to which he has had access] owing to his position as a person who holds or has held a contract made on behalf of His Majesty, or as a person who is or has been employed under a person who holds or has held such an office or contract –

(a)   communicates the [code word, pass word,] sketch, plan or model, article, note, document, or information to any person, other than a person to whom he is authorised to communicate it, or,

[(aa) Uses the information in his possession for the benefit of any foreign power or in any other manner prejudicial to the safety or interests of the State;]

(b)   retains the sketch, plan, model, article, note, or document in his possession or control when he has no right to retain it or when it is contrary to his duty to retain it [or fails to comply with all directions issued by lawful authority with regard to the return or disposal thereof] [or

(c)   fails to take reasonable care of, or so conducts himself as to endanger the safety of the sketch, plan, model, article, note, document, secret official code or pass word or information]:

that person shall be guilty of a misdemeanour.

[(1A) If any person having in his possession or control any sketch, plan, model, article, note, document, or information which relates to munitions of war, communicates it directly or indirectly to any foreign power, or in any other manner prejudicial to the safety or interests of the State, that person shall be guilty of a misdemeanour;]

(2) If any person receives any [secret official code word, or password, or] sketch, plan, model, article, note, document, or information, knowing, or having reasonable ground to believe, at the time when he receives it, that the [code word, pass word] sketch, plan, model, article, note, document, or information is communicated to him in contravention of this Act, he shall be guilty of a misdemeanour, unless he proves that the communication to him of the [code word, pass word,] sketch, plan, model, article, note, document, or information was contrary to his desire.

Well, that is bad drafting, even by legal standards. One piece of evidence to the Franks Committee in 1971–2 suggested that this Section produced over 2000 possible charges. The Franks Committee in their report provided an excellent analysis of the main features of the Section. Clearly (or perhaps not so clearly!) the main offence created by Section 2 is the unauthorised communication of official information by a Crown servant. *The important point though is that this is not limited to classified or secret information. Every piece of official information is covered.* As the Franks Committee said:.

> The leading characteristic of this offence is its catch-all quality. It catches all official documents and inform- ation. It makes no distinction of kind, and no distinction of degree. All information which a Crown servant learns in the course of his duty is 'official' for the purposes of Section 2, whatever its nature, whatever its importance, whatever its original source. A blanket is thrown over everything; nothing escapes. The Section catches all Crown servants as well as official information.

But Government simply could not function on this basis since there obviously has to be some release of information. The key word is 'authorisation'. If communication of information is authorised then it is not an offence. Again, as Franks says, the actual process of 'authorisation' is far from clear:

> Actual practice within the Government rests heavily on a doctrine of implied authorisation... Ministers are, in effect, self-authorising. They decide for themselves what to reveal. Senior civil servants exercise a considerable degree of personal judgement in deciding what disclosures of official information they may properly make, and to whom.

This concept of 'authorisation' makes possible the whole Whitehall ethos of providing information as we shall see later in the chapter. Put briefly, a 'background brief', 'lobby briefing', 'off-the-record' discussion are in practice 'author-ised' communications for the purposes of Section 2; 'leaks' are, of course, by Government definition 'unauthorised' and therefore potential criminal offences.

But Section 2 does provide another way in which communication of information is not an offence under the 1911 Act. That is when the communication is to 'a person to whom it is in the interests of the State his duty to communicate it'. Franks commented in 1972 that the meaning of the words was 'obscure'. These were the words that formed the basis of the defence I put forward at the Old Bailey to the charge of communicating information to an MP in circumstances where the Government was misleading Parliament. Although we undertook extensive research into legal precedent this was, as far as we could see, the first time such a defence had been made to an Official Secrets Act charge. It was moreover the first time anybody had been charged for passing information to an MP.

There are other important aspects to Section 2 that are worth highlighting. First, it does not apply only to Crown servants. Also included are Government contractors and others entrusted with information so that a 'chain' of offences can be constructed. Second, Section 2(2) makes the mere receipt of official information an offence. Third, *mens rea* or guilty knowledge is a vital part of nearly all criminal offences. Section 2(2) clearly has this element, although Section 2(1)(a) which creates the offences of unauthorised communication does not contain any wording to make it clear whether *mens rea* is or is not an ingredient of any offence. Judicial rulings have given different decisions. In my case the judge very strongly ruled out *mens rea* as a defence.

There is a further aspect of the operation of Section 2 that needs to be considered. Because of the way in which it is drafted Section 2 means that most civil servants probably commit a technical breach of the law every day. They tell their families or friends ('unauthorised persons') about some aspect of their work or information gained in the course of their work – that they went to a meeting, met the Minister or wrote a letter. (Or that 'old chestnut' of Civil Service jokes about revealing the quality of the lavatory paper.)

How then is it decided which of the thousands of offences committed every day should be prosecuted? Section 8 of the Official Secrets Act provides that no prosecution can be brought without the consent of the Attorney-General. This probably stops frivolous prosecutions but causes other problems. The Attorney-General is first and foremost a politician and a member of the Government (though not the Cabinet). Yet he is also expected to exercise his discretion in Official Secrets Act cases independently – in his capacity as the senior Law Officer and not as a politician – and reach a conclusion about the 'public interest' in bringing a prosecution. This clearly must be a difficult role for any politician to carry out. But in addition the way in which the Attorney-General exercises his power of discretion is not open to challenge. His decision is final. The position of the Attorney-General can obviously be used to ensure that no prosecution is brought that is against the interests of the Government of the day. But what happens to his consideration of the 'public interest' if a possible offence has damaged the political interests of the Government or exposed some form of malpractice? The Attorney-General might decide to prosecute in order to protect the reputation of his political colleagues. His discretion could not be challenged and the Official Secrets Act is drafted so widely that there would be a very good chance of a successful prosecution.

Many distinguished and experienced commentators have recognised that the Official Secrets Act can be used 'politically' by the Government against those who have embarrassed them in some way. In a letter to *The Times* in May 1928 J.H. Morgan KC, a well-known constitutional lawyer, made a particularly telling indictment of this highly undesirable use of the law. He wrote that the Official Secrets Act:

> Put into the hands of the bureaucracy the power to prevent, or threaten to prevent, anyone who has ever served the Crown, however temporarily, from dis-

closing, after he has left the Service, to the public, in the interests of national safety, facts which such a person may have discovered by the exercise of his own wits and as the result of his own investigations, which he has himself reported to the Department he served, which have been deliberately suppressed by it and which the same Department may have as deliberately concealed from the House of Commons even to the extent of telling the House, in reply to Parliamentary questions, carefully conceived Departmental falsehoods. I have known such a case. *The Act, or rather a certain section of it, is the most vicious Act ever devised by Government Departments to protect themselves against the consequences of their own chicanery, and at the same time to deceive the public and intimidate the Press.* [Italics added.]

Forty-five years later similar fears were expressed to the Franks Committee by Mr Justice Caulfield who had been the judge in the highly political Official Secrets Act trial the previous year of Jonathan Aitken and the *Daily Telegraph* over the publication of a report about the Nigerian civil war. Caulfield said:

I could add many other worries I have about this Section but perhaps it is sufficient to say that *I think the Section in its present form could be viciously or capriciously used by an embarrassed executive.* [Italics added.]

Others were also concerned about this very point. In their report the Franks Committee argued that:

A number of witnesses pointed out that Section 2 could be used to serve the political interests of a Government, or to save Ministers or officials from embarrassment. No witness suggested that this was a proper use of the criminal law. We reject entirely the use of criminal sanctions for such purposes.

How Section 2 has been used
The first known case brought about under Section 2 was in

May 1916 when two people were both sentenced to two months' imprisonment. One was a clerk in the War Office who had passed information, much of it highly critical of senior officials, to the second person who published it in the *Military Mail*. A more important trial took place in 1919. Again it concerned a clerk in the War Office. This individual had passed information about contracts for Army officers' clothing to the secretary of a firm of tailors. The defence argued that Section 2 could only be used in cases where the information could be useful to an enemy. The Westminster magistrate accepted this interpretation and dismissed the charges. Realising that this decision would have severely limited the scope of Section 2 the Attorney-General intervened, and on a bill of indictment a trial took place. Mr Justice Amory refused to restrict the scope of Section 2 and both men were fined. It was made clear that Section 2 had indeed been drafted in such a way that it did cover all official information whatever its nature.

Just how widely the Act had been drawn was demonstrated by the next three cases. At the end of 1926 a former Governor of Pentonville Prison, Major Blake, was tried at the Old Bailey for publishing an article in the *Evening News* called 'What Bywaters Said To Me', which was supposed to be the confession of a murderer shortly before his execution. The defence argued that Section 2 should only apply to disclosures that were prejudicial to the State. Again this attempt to limit the scope of Section 2 failed and Major Blake was fined £250. In 1932 a clerk in the Principal Probate Registry gave a journalist information about the wills of three famous people that were to be made public later in the day. The clerk was sentenced to imprisonment for six weeks and the journalist for two months. A year later the well-known author Compton McKenzie pleaded guilty at the Old Bailey after he had written a manuscript of a book drawing on information he had obtained during the war as a Royal Marine officer.

The next year there was a more controversial case which was one of the many that involved the selective prosecution of those concerned. Edgar Lansbury, the son of the Labour party leader George Lansbury, was convicted and fined £20 at Bow Street Magistrates Court on charges under Section 2(2) of the Act. Edgar Lansbury had been writing a biography of his father and had used material derived from two Cabinet papers dating from the second Labour Government in 1930 and 1931. The Government took the case so seriously that the Attorney-General, Sir Thomas Inskip, personally conducted the prosecution. But since Edgar Lansbury could only have got the documents from his father the latter had obviously committed an offence under Section 2(1). However, the Government simply could not face the prospect of putting the Leader of the Opposition on trial and so no prosecution was brought against him.

During the 1930's there were three cases where the use or threatened use of Section 6 of the 1920 Act proved to be highly controversial. The last of these involving a Member of Parliament led to the only reform in the hundred-year history of the Official Secrets Act.

Section 6 was contentious because it required every person to give any information in his power about an offence, or even a suspected offence, under the 1911 and 1920 Acts. Failure to do so would be a criminal offence. Journalists naturally suspected that the power might be used to require them to reveal their sources. The Attorney-General, Sir Gordon Hewart, had assured the House of Commons in 1920 that Section 6 would only be used in cases of spying. But it had been written in such a way that it covered possible Section 2 offences. It was not long before the Government started to use the available power. In 1930 there was a 'leak' in three newspapers about a Cabinet decision to arrest the Indian leader Mahatma Gandhi. The police were called in and started to question the journalists and the proprietors of the newspapers concerned. The inquiry was called off after it was made clear by the newspapers that any proceedings would reveal the Cabinet Minister who had been responsible for the 'leak'! The investigations produced a storm of protests from the Press and as a result assurances were again obtained from the Government about the use of Section 6.

The next case involved a journalist, a Mr Lewis of the Manchester *Daily Despatch*, who published a description of a wanted man which was clearly based on a police circular. He was not charged under Section 2 but when he refused to reveal the source of his information he was charged under Section 6, found guilty and fined £5. This episode showed that the assurances given in 1920 and 1930 were valueless and demands were made for the amendment of the 1920 Act. These were rejected by the Home Secretary and a Private Members' Bill to amend the law failed. But Dingle Foot, who introduced the Bill and had earlier described the Official Secrets Acts as 'a sort of statutory monstrosity', warned the House of Commons about the use of Section 6 and claimed that 'nothing quite like it exists anywhere else in the whole range of our criminal law'. It was to take one more attempted use of Section 6 before it was reformed.

The Sandys Affair

In 1938 Duncan Sandys, the Conservative MP for Norwood, was also an officer in the Territorial Army. In this role he had discovered considerable details about the deficient state of anti-aircraft defences for London. He wrote to Hore-Belisha, the Secretary of State for War, stating what he had found out and giving him a draft parliamentary question which Sandys intended to table. The Prime Minister, Neville Chamberlain, was later to claim that what happened next was 'a most extraordinary catalogue of misunderstandings'. Duncan Sandys' letter was passed down through the War Office and the military were appalled not at what it revealed but that Sandys knew about it. They protested to Hore-Belisha about the fact that a junior TA officer had got hold of this information. Hore-Belisha went to see Chamberlain. It was decided to call in the Attorney-General, Sir Donald Somervell, who sent for Duncan Sandys. Sandys told the House of Commons that the Attorney-General had asked him to reveal his sources and continued 'when I enquired what would be the consequences were I to refuse to comply with the request he read me the text of Section 6 of the Official Secrets Act and pointed out that I might render myself liable to a term of imprisonment not exceeding two years'. The Attorney-General later tried to claim that he had not intended to make any threats.

Nevertheless the actions of the Government were almost certainly a major breach of parliamentary privilege. A committee was set up to investigate. Its report tended to play down the issue, but the Commons decided to set up another committee to investigate the use of the Official Secrets Act in cases involving Members of Parliament. Many of the speakers, including the Leader of the Opposition, Clem Attlee, and the Liberal leader, Sir Archibald Sinclair, commented on the inability of the Government to tell the difference between their own interests and the wider national interest. But the most ringing denunciation of the Government was left to Sir Winston Churchill:

> The Official Secrets Act was devised to protect the national defences and ought not to be used to shield Ministers who may have neglected the national defences. *It ought not to be used to shield Ministers who have strong personal interests in concealing the truth about matters from the country* [italics added]. I am taking the case that if there were a Minister who had strong reasons to believe that he would be convicted of inefficiency, he would have a strong interest in preventing the disclosure of facts which would support that charge.

The Official Secrets Act of 1939

The Committee started work in the autumn of 1938 and reported in April 1939. The crucial point for debate was the question of parliamentary privilege and in particular the privilege enshrined in the Bill of Rights of 1688 which formed part of the great constitutional settlement when William III gained the throne in the 'Glorious Revolution':

> That the freedom of speech and debates or proceedings

in Parliament ought not to be impeached or questioned in any court or place out of Parliament.

The Committee were clear that 'proceedings in Parliament' had to be interpreted widely so as to include most of the duties of a Member of Parliament. The Committee also considered the question of the provision of information to a Member of Parliament and they argued that disclosure 'in the interests of the State' (as in Section 2 of the Official Secrets Act) could provide protection, and that whether any such action fell within those terms would be a matter for the jury at any trial to decide, and that the Government would not have the final say in the matter. The Committee went on to say:

A measure of protection is thus afforded to any person who communicates information to a Member of Parliament.

The Committee also criticised the Official Secrets Act and the way it could constrain MPs:

The Acts, if strictly enforced, would make it difficult for Members to obtain the information without which they cannot effectively discharge their duty. Any action which, without actually infringing any privilege enjoyed by Members of the House in their capacity as Members, yet obstructs or impedes them in the discharge of their duties, or tends to produce such results, even though the act be lawful, may be held to be a contempt of the House.

By the time the report was ready the Government, which had meanwhile set up their own Ministerial committee, had decided to legislate. The Official Secrets Act of 1939 provided that the interrogation powers of Section 6 should only apply to offences or suspected offences under Section 1 of the 1911 Act, or in other words only in espionage cases. It was a small step back from the widespread powers granted by the Official Secrets Acts and it had only been achieved because of the involvement of a Member of Parliament in possible prosecution under the Acts.

The Discrediting of Section 2

After the Second World War a steady stream of prosecutions were brought, most of them about relatively trivial disclosures including Government contracts, police inform- ation given to journalists and retention of documents. One of the most famous cases was in 1958 when two Oxford undergraduates were prosecuted for an article they had published in the University magazine *Isis*. The article was based on their national service experience in the Royal Navy. It dealt with provocative incidents on the Soviet frontier and the use made of the incidents by signals interception stations. There was a lengthy *in camera* trial in which the Solicitor-General prosecuted. Both men were found guilty and were sentenced to three months' imprisonment, but in the true tradition of the British establishment – and despite the international and security implications of the article – it was directed that the sentences should be served in comfortable circumstances and away from 'criminals'.

One of the most controversial of all Official Secrets Acts cases came in 1971; it led to the trial judge saying that Section 2 should be 'pensioned off' and replaced by a measure which would provide greater clarity about what actions were likely to lead to prosecution. The case arose from events during the Nigerian civil war. The decision by the British Government to support the Nigerian Federal Government by supplying arms to help defeat the Biafran rebels was a highly controversial and emotional subject. A confidential report by the Defence Adviser at the High Commission in Lagos (Colonel Scott) passed through two unofficial hands before it reached Jonathan Aitken, a journalist, and also a prospective Conservative parliamentary candidate. It was also handled by a Conservative MP, Hugh Fraser, before it was passed to the *Sunday Telegraph* which printed extracts. The report seemed to show that statements by Government Ministers in the House of Commons were inaccurate about the amount of arms supplied by the British Government.

The Government called in the police to investigate and eventually a number of people in the chain of those who had handled the document were prosecuted – Colonel Cairns, who had received a copy of the report from the Defence Adviser in Nigeria, Jonathan Aitken, and the editor of the *Sunday Telegraph*. General Alexander, who had acted as intermediary between Cairns and Aitken, was not prosecuted and he turned into a major prosecution witness. Hugh Fraser was not prosecuted but wrote to *The Times* demanding to be prosecuted. The prosecution could not prove that all those involved believed they were committing offences and after a long trial lasting about a fortnight the jury acquitted all the accused. Because of the weakness of the prosecution case the defendants had only to sketch in outline a public interest defence in publishing the information. The full implications of a defence based on the 'interests of the State' had to wait until my own trial nearly fifteen years later.

An equally controversial trial took place in the mid 1970's, known as the ABC trial from the names of the three defendants, Crispin Aubrey, John Berry and Duncan Campbell. Aubrey and Campbell were journalists who had gone to a flat in north London to talk to an ex-soldier, John Berry, who had worked at signals interception stations in Cyprus. They had tape-recorded the interview and as they left the flat all three were arrested by members of Special Branch, almost certainly alerted to the fact that the meeting was to take place from information gained by telephone tapping. As the prosecution put the case together more and more charges were laid against the three defendants, culminating in charges under Section 1 (the espionage section) for the accumulation of information which, although in itself not classified, would when put together be useful to an enemy.

The first trial at the Old Bailey ran into trouble at the start. It was suddenly discovered that the jury had been vetted. The first jury had to be discharged after it was revealed on a TV programme that the foreman was an ex-member of the SAS. Then the judge fell ill and had to be replaced. The trial rapidly disintegrated in the hands of the prosecution. Witness after witness gave evidence that various stations and establishments were highly secret only for the defence to show that the information was publicly available. The judge virtually directed the prosecution to drop the Section 1 charges. Others were dropped later. Eventually the jury convicted all three defendants under Section 2 but the judge only imposed a suspended sentence on Berry and conditional discharges on Aubrey and Campbell. The trial was widely seen as a triumph for the three defendants and their lawyers and a disaster for the Government in completely misjudging the case. Coming after the Nigerian case the Official Secrets Act seemed to be totally discredited.

But it was wheeled out again in the trial at the Old Bailey of Sarah Tisdall. She was a clerk in the private office of Sir Geoffrey Howe, the Foreign Secretary, and she had photocopied two minutes from the Defence Secretary, Michael Heseltine, to the Prime Minister and sent them to the *Guardian*. The two minutes dealt with the arrangements for the arrival of US cruise missiles at the RAF base at Greenham Common and the way in which it was proposed to handle statements to Parliament. When the *Guardian* published one document and part of another the Government swung into action to try and recover the documents and trace the leak. After a major legal battle the *Guardian* made a highly controversial decision to hand back the documents rather than destroy them, enabling the police to charge Sarah Tisdall. At the Old Bailey she pleaded guilty and was sentenced to six months' imprisonment. The unexpected severity of the sentence provoked virtually universal condemnation.

The Thatcher Government, continually plagued by 'leaks' of various kinds from the Civil Service, had clearly decided to call in the police at every opportunity and prosecute whenever possible on the assumption that the 'public interest' was best served by 'deterrence'. No doubt the successful prosecution of Sarah Tisdall only emboldened Ministers to prosecute me for the leak of the *Belgrano* papers to Tam Dalyell regardless of the very different circumstances.

Whitehall and the Culture of Secrecy

Why are the Government and the Civil Service so obsessed by secrecy and the punishment of leaks? Why are they set against introducing a Freedom of Information Act which would do away with most leaks? Why are there so many leaks under all Governments? Much of the explanation lies deeply buried in the culture of Whitehall and its devotion to closed Government. The cement that holds the closed world of Whitehall together is the Official Secrets Acts.

The first event that happens in the career of every civil servant, whether they are budding mandarins, gardeners, clerks, car drivers, cooks or cleaners, is that they are asked to sign an Official Secrets Act form known as E74. This form says:

OFFICIAL SECRETS ACTS

Declaration To be signed by members of Government Departments on appointment and, where desirable, by non-civil servants on first being given access to Government information.

My attention has been drawn to the provisions of the Official Secrets Acts set out on the back of this document and I am fully aware of the serious consequences which may follow any breach of those provisions.

I understand that the Sections of the Official Secrets Acts set out on the back of this document cover material published in a speech, lecture, or radio or television broadcast, or in the Press or in book form. I am aware that I should not divulge any information gained by me as a result of my appointment to any unauthorised person, either orally or in writing, without the previous official sanction in writing of the Department appointing me, to which written application should be made and two copies of the proposed publication be forwarded.

I understand also that I am liable to be prosecuted if I publish without official sanction any information I may acquire in the course of my tenure of an official appointment (unless it has already officially been made public) or retain without official sanction any sketch, plan, model, article, note or official documents which are no longer needed for my official duties, and that these provisions apply not only during the period of my appointment but also after my appointment has ceased. I also understand that I must surrender any documents, etc, referred to in section 2(1) of the Act if I am transferred from one post to another, save such as have been issued to me for my personal retention.

There are two interesting points about this form. First, it has no legal standing. Everybody is bound by the Official Secrets Acts whether they sign the form or not. Second, it is misleading. The text of the Official Secrets Acts is set out on the back of the form. The front part, where every civil servant has to sign, has nothing to do with the Official Secrets Acts. The requirement to submit two copies of any publication for official clearance is a purely administrative measure and has no legal backing. No doubt it is thought convenient to try and give the impression that this is a legal requirement. These forms have considerable symbolic value and the prosecution at my own trial thought it was important to include a copy of the form I had signed nearly fifteen years before as evidence that I knew that I was breaking the law in sending the papers to Tam Dalyell.

So the first event in a civil servant's life is to read the Official Secrets Acts. As soon as a civil servant starts a job in Whitehall the overwhelming importance of secrecy rapidly becomes apparent. There are many different classifications each with their own set of special procedures for handling documents, which have to be signed for and recorded in special books. If they are highly classified then a receipt has to be obtained every time the document changes hands. There is a highly elaborate system within Whitehall for classifying documents which is, in theory, based on the damage that their release would cause to the nation. There are four basic security categories ranging from 'Restricted', through 'Confidential' and 'Secret' to 'Top Secret'. The official definition about their release is:

Restricted: undesirable in the interests of the nation
Confidential: prejudicial in the interests of the nation
Secret: serious injury to the interests of the nation
Top Secret: exceptionally grave damage to the nation.

In addition there are categories such as 'Commercial-in-Confidence', 'Staff-in-Confidence', 'Management-in-Confidence' to cover other information. Although the official definitions purport to make clear distinctions, in practice it is very difficult to decide exactly how documents should be classified and most of the time it is a matter of judgement or following previous practice. This system has nothing to do with Section 2 and the Official Secrets Acts which cover, as we have already seen, all official information. As the Franks Committee put it:

Security classification is a purely administrative system, unrelated to the criminal law ... classification does not determine the sanctions taken for unauthorised disclosure.

This system creates an atmosphere and pervasive belief inside Whitehall that because the information is classified it must therefore be important. More subtly it helps to create in civil servants the view that they are important people because they are privileged enough to have access to this information. They are insiders. Everybody else is by definition an outsider and the information others have, whilst perhaps interesting, is not 'official' and is therefore not important. Under this system more significance will automatically be attached to an 'official' analysis of say, a country's economic or defence policy, than to any information from 'outsiders', however distinguished or experienced. This serves to reinforce the view of the Civil Service as the closed and charmed circle. Most top civil servants subscribe to a view, although it is not often articulated, that closed government is good government. They would claim that a closed decision taking system is better because it is more rational. The Civil Service, as the guardians of the State, are able, it would be argued, to analyse a problem objectively and, free from illegitimate outside pressure, reach the best solution in the interests of the nation as a whole. Secrecy is therefore the cement that holds Whitehall together, the one common interest of all Government Departments.

This secretive atmosphere leads to a very claustrophobic world. Top mandarins normally spend their whole careers in Whitehall, often entirely in one Ministry. They may have contact with outside bodies but they have little or no experience of life outside Whitehall. Their world is one of Ministerial meetings and policy-making inside Whitehall. This limited view of the world from Whitehall makes life in that small part of London all important. Battles between departments, protecting themselves from outside attack, is all that matters. Policy-making thus becomes a great mystery which cannot and must not be exposed to outsiders who have no right to know how this activity is carried on.

William Plowden, the Director of the Royal Institute of Public Administration and a former Under-Secretary in Whitehall, has described brilliantly the effect of this closed world on the way in which Whitehall and the Civil Service actually works:

> They develop, like any kind of closed profession, a culture and a language of their own. They communicate with each other in terms that they understand; phrases like 'at the end of the day', 'ball's in your court', 'a sticky wicket' are used inside the Civil Service. And I think the sorts of argument they use are phrased in terms which they recognise and which convey their meaning to each other, but which wouldn't carry so much conviction with an outside audience ... The thing about the language of Whitehall is that it makes it unnecessary very often to carry arguments right through to the end, because so many assumptions are shared. It's not so much the language as the culture really. So many assumptions are shared that one doesn't need to argue every point out in detail in the way you would if you were

trying to persuade a hostile or certainly critical outside audience.

In a different vein, it is the exposure of this mentality and jargon that has made the TV programme *Yes Minister* so successful.

This method of working has another consequence. Some groups and special interests are branded as legitimate, others as illegitimate. Most senior civil servants would never regard Whitehall departments as special interest groups lobbying within the system. Yet that is exactly what they are and how they behave. Their power often depends on the general political climate or the strength of their Minister, but they carefully protect themselves from outside enquiry and are greatly heartened when they score a 'victory' on some policy over their 'enemies' whether it is the Treasury or some other department. Moreover, within departments themselves, particularly in the case of the Ministry of Defence, there are competing special interest groups trying in turn to protect themselves and obtain greater influence and more resources. Inside MOD there has always been a continuous battle between the Armed Services, and they lose no opportunity to score points off each other.

The process of 'legitimising' interest groups is of course obscure, but the effects are obvious. The DHSS would not even consider making changes in the Health Service without consulting the British Medical Association. At times the Ministry of Agriculture seems to be little more than an extension of the National Farmers Union. The Treasury pays great attention to the views of the Bank of England. These bodies are, however, not seen as pressure groups. They are regarded as legitimate and responsible bodies, part of the establishment in its widest sense, whose views must be taken into account. Other groups which represent the views of (often large) sections of the general public are meanwhile regarded as somehow illegitimate and irresponsible. They do not need to be consulted; they may occasionally be thrown a small concession if they can manage to create so much political pressure that Ministers are worried that they may lose votes on the issue.

Secrecy also conditions the Whitehall climate about the provision of information. Information is seen as something to be controlled by Whitehall and allowed outside only when it is politically convenient. We can find evidence of this in the newspapers every day. Ministers will tell the media what went on in Cabinet meetings within minutes of the end of the meeting. Journalists are fed large chunks of Cabinet papers; descriptions of battles between Ministers are carefully planted with friendly journalists. Ministers see themselves as self-authorised to reveal the information. This attitude, together with the lobby system of 'off-the-record' and 'unattributable' briefings where the Government line is fed to the waiting journalists who then print it, is suitably disguised as coming from 'sources close to the Prime Minister' (the No. 10 Press Secretary), 'senior Government sources' (a Cabinet Minister) etc. For a great deal of the time the flow of information is in the hands of the Government. Thus when Whitehall justifies not having a Freedom of Information Act by saying that more information is being made available all it really means is that the public relations effort is increasing.

Whitehall is very concerned to keep the flow of information under control. Outside bodies are entitled only to receive the minimum amount of information possible. Parliament and MPs are generally regarded as being 'outside'. There is an adversarial relationship with the Government doing all it can to give away as little as possible in parliamentary questions and debates.

Secrecy is at the core of Whitehall. It is not therefore surprising that the Civil Service as a body is against greater openness in Government and reform of the Official Secrets Acts. If this happened the power of the Civil Service would be drastically reduced and so would the power of those interest groups that are close to the Civil Service. Politicians would also be subject to greater scrutiny and the mysteries of policy-making would be disclosed to profane eyes. The Civil

Service has therefore, in alliance with politicians, blocked reform of the Official Secrets Acts and the introduction of Freedom of Information legislation. How they did it is the subject of the next chapter.

CHAPTER TWO

THE BLOCKING OF REFORM

Over the past twenty years there has been growing pressure for the reform of Section 2 of the Official Secrets Act and also for its replacement by a Freedom of Information measure. A large number of Bills has been introduced in Parliament to achieve one or both of these ends. There has been a prestigious Government enquiry chaired by one of the most exalted members of the 'establishment' – Lord Franks – which recommended wholesale reform. Governments have entered office with manifesto promises to implement reform. Legislation has been promised in three Queen's Speeches at the opening of a new Parliamentary session. But absolutely nothing has been achieved. Why?

As we saw in the first chapter there is a close identity of interest between politicians and the Civil Service in seeing that reform is blocked. Politicians can see the attractions of greater openness when in opposition. Once in power their views start to change. Why should they give their opponents access to more information which can be used for political purposes? News manipulation through officially inspired 'background briefings' (or 'leaks') seems much more attractive. The legislative programme is always tightly constrained for time so why fill it up with this reform when there are so many other measures that are more politically attractive? Ministers are encouraged in this view by the Civil Service. The department responsible for policy on the Official Secrets Act is the Home Office, never one of the most dynamic and reformist ministries. There is no real pressure from within Whitehall for reform. Reform of Section 2 may be needed, it is argued, but what do we put in its place? Long studies are always required and the supposed cost of running a Freedom of Information statute can always be introduced into the argument if necessary. Change in the existing situation will upset the hermetic world of Whitehall and introduce outside pressures and unruly voices into the cosy atmosphere between Ministers and civil servants. It will certainly weaken the influence of the latter. Whitehall is expert at foot-dragging when required and on this subject it has been tacitly, and sometimes openly, encouraged by Ministers. As a result all attempts at reform have been blocked. Just how has this been achieved since the mid 1960's?

The debate about secrecy and the use of the Official Secrets Act stemmed initially not from the use of the Act but from the imprisonment of two journalists who refused to disclose their sources to the judicial Tribunal investigating the Vassall spy case. Early in 1964 'Justice' (the British section of the International Commission of Jurists) and the British Committee of the International Press Institute set up a joint working party on 'The Law and the Press'. Obviously the working party included the Official Secrets Act in their study. Their report, published in 1965, recommended that Section 2 should be limited in scope by introducing the defence that the communication or receipt of official information had not been likely to harm either the national interest or private interests entrusted to the State. The next year there was a debate in the House of Lords on the report and a number of Private Members' Bills were introduced in Parliament but none made much progress.

The Fulton Report (1968)

In 1966 the Prime Minister, Harold Wilson, asked an old friend, Lord Fulton (they had been temporary civil servants together during the Second World War), to head an enquiry into the Civil Service. Fulton was, in 1966, vice-Chancellor of the University of Sussex and he shared views with Harold Wilson about lack of drive and originality in the Civil Service and its domination by the arts educated, Oxbridge, generalist administrator. (I am only guilty of the first and last of these crimes.) The report, when it was published in 1968, was radical; it recommended wholesale reform and the ending of what it described as the domination of 'the philosophy of the amateur'. The Government immediately accepted the main recommendations. The fact that most of those recommendations have never seriously been introduced is the best example of the power of the Whitehall bureaucracy to divert, delay and eventually stop any reform which it does not like or which threatens its own status, interests or methods of conducting business.

However the Fulton Committee also considered the question of secrecy in Whitehall which it thought was excessive:

> The increasingly wide range of problems handled by Government, and their far-reaching effects upon the community as a whole, demand the widest possible consultation with its different parts and interests . . . It is healthy for a democracy increasingly to press to be consulted and informed. There are still too many occasions when information is unnecessarily withheld and consultation merely perfunctory . . . It is an abuse of consultation when it is turned into a belated attempt to prepare the ground for decisions that in reality have been taken already.

As if to illustrate that the Fulton committee had analysed the situation correctly the Wilson Government published in 1969 a White Paper: 'Information and the Public Interest'. The Government had carried out an enquiry into secrecy recommended by Fulton but it had been 'on a wide inter-departmental basis' only – no consultation with outside interests. Here we have Whitehall telling itself that everything is all right. The report made the bold claim that it had studied 'comprehensively both the existing trend and its possible future development'. It concluded complacently that more information was being published (a plea to be repeated by the Thatcher Government fifteen years later) but neglected to mention that much of this was not 'information' as such but rather public relations work by the Government.

Towards the end of the report there was a passage about the Official Secrets Acts which said that there was a case for protecting much official information from unauthorised disclosure and that a criminal sanction was required for the protection of some of this official information. It then went on to state that the Official Secrets Acts were not a barrier to greater openness since they did not stop the 'authorised' release of information in any way. This report encapsulates the official Whitehall view of official secrecy and freedom of information, a view that has not changed since 1969. The Official Secrets Acts should be retained as they are because even if they are archaic they can still be useful in protecting Whitehall and in preserving the idea that 'information' is what Whitehall chooses to give out and not what people are entitled to know.

The Heath Government

A new Conservative Government entered office in June 1970 with a manifesto pledge to eliminate unnecessary secrecy in the workings of Government and set up a review of the operation of the Official Secrets Act. That review had to wait until the conclusion of the *Daily Telegraph* secrets trial in February 1971 when, as we have seen in the previous chapter, all the defendants were acquitted and the judge, Mr Justice Caulfield, suggested in his summing up that Section 2 of the 1911 Act should be 'pensioned off'. A committee was set up by the Home Secretary in April 1971 'to review the operation of Section 2 of the Official Secrets Act 1911 and to make recommendations'. It was chaired by one of the highest ranking of 'The Great and the Good' – those that Whitehall uses to run and sit on enquiries and committees – Lord Franks. He had had a distinguished public career and was later to be asked by Mrs Thatcher to chair the enquiry into the origins of the Falklands conflict. Other members of the committee drawn from suitable sub-categories of 'The Great and the Good' list included Sir Patrick Dean, from the political world, William Deedes (now editor of the *Daily Telegraph*, then a Tory MP), Merlyn Rees, Brian Walden and from the media Ian Trethowan.

The Franks Report 1972

The report contained a long and detailed analysis of the operation of Section 2, the cases brought under it and how it had been drafted. It presented major and comprehensive recommendations for reform. For an 'establishment' committee its comments were hard-hitting:

> We found Section 2 a mess. Its scope is enormously wide. Any law which impinges on the freedom of information in a democracy should be much more tightly drawn. A catch-all provision is saved from absurdity in operation only by the sparing exercise of the Attorney-General's discretion to prosecute. Yet the very width of this discretion, and the inevitably selective way in which it is exercised, gives rise to considerable unease. The drafting and interpretation of the Section are obscure. People are not sure what it means, or how it operates in practice, or what kinds of action involve real risk of prosecution under it.

They went on to comment on the inevitable but unfortunate linkage between Section 1 dealing with spying, and Section 2. The Franks Committee said of Section 2:

> It deals with information of all kinds, and it catches people who have no thought of harming their country. Many consider it wrong that such a provision should appear side by side with the rest of the Official Secrets Acts.

The conclusion they came to was that 'these factors convinced us that change was essential'.

The Committee went on to consider what changes should be introduced. The first conclusion was that Section 2 should be repealed and replaced by narrower and more specific provisions in a new Official Information Act.

The main proposal was to limit strictly the area of information covered by the criminal law. In the words of the report, 'A section which has been described as an ancient blunderbuss, scattering shot in all directions, needs replacement by a modern weapon'. The proposal was that the proper basis for the employment of criminal sanctions should be limited to 'the unauthorised disclosure of official information which would be likely to cause serious injury to the security of the nation or the safety of the people'. On the current definitions for the classification of information this would mean SECRET or above. As this meant bringing the purely administrative Civil Service system of security classification into the criminal law, a system was obviously required to ensure that information in any unauthorised disclose had been properly classified. Franks proposed that before a decision was taken to prosecute there should be a review by the responsible Minister who would be required to consider whether, at the time of the disclosure, the information was properly classified. Other information not covered by the Official Information Act would, as a consequence, be protected, not by possible criminal sanctions, but by Civil Service disciplinary procedures. In addition the receipt of official information would no longer be a criminal offence.

These fundamental proposals were agreed by a distinguished group of people drawn from the establishment. Yet despite the clear evidence that the provisions and operation of Section 2 no longer commanded confidence the 1972 proposals have never been implemented. The highly unsatisfactory position devastatingly analysed by Lord Franks and his colleagues has remained completely unchanged. The Conservative Government having commissioned the report took nine months to consider its response.

The process of delay had started. In June 1973, the then Home Secretary, Robert Carr, said that the Government accepted the essential recommendations made by Lord Franks but it would also wish to consider further categories of information to be protected. The normal Whitehall process of nibbling away at the recommendations made by reports was underway. Nothing more was heard of the subject for the remaining life of the Heath Government.

A Freedom of Information Act?

After the February election in 1974 Labour returned to power and within a month, on 2 April, the Prime Minister, Harold Wilson, said: 'I hope to give an answer . . . in a shorter time than the previous Government.' Most of the debate so far had been about reform of Section 2 and restricting the scope of the criminal law. A new element now emerged – Freedom of Information. The USA and a number of other countries had passed legislation which provided a statutory right for citizens to obtain information. This was of course a very different proposition from restricting the prosecution of civil servants to cases involving highly classified information. It was seized on as a golden opportunity for Whitehall opponents of reform to introduce new delaying tactics. Clearly, they argued, we cannot proceed with piecemeal reform, we must first study the wider proposals. But this would, of course, take time.

In the summer of 1974 an internal Labour party study, 'People and the Media', floated the idea of a public right of access to official information. The proposal found a place in the October 1974 election manifesto:

> Labour believes that the process of government should be more open to the public. We shall: Replace the Official Secrets Act by a measure to put the burden on the public authorities to justify withholding information.

In Harold Wilson's second administration a Cabinet committee – MISC 89 – chaired by the Home Secretary, Roy Jenkins, was set up to consider what to do. The first step was to go to Washington and see how Freedom of Information worked.

In their book *The Civil Servants: An Inquiry into Britain's Ruling Class*, Peter Kellner and Lord Crowther-Hunt describe what happened next. Lord Crowther-Hunt was in a good position to know since he was a Minister in the Labour Government dealing with constitutional issues.

Jenkins' visit to Washington in January 1975, with Sir Arthur Peterson, his Permanent Secretary, and Anthony Lester, his special adviser, could scarcely have taken place at a worse time. The Freedom of Information Act had only recently been strengthened, over an attempted veto by President Ford, and against the wishes of the Justice Department. Although it was too early to tell, a number of officials in the American administration informed Jenkins and his colleagues that the newly amended Act would be expensive to administer, and employ extra civil servants. And because the new Act was so young, its supporters did not yet have evidence to counter the Justice Department's assertions. Jenkins returned to London and announced his fears that a British Freedom of Information Act would be 'costly, cumbersome and legalistic'.

With growing lack of enthusiasm MISC 89 continued its work. Proposals for amending Section 2 were still very much on the table and at one meeting of Permanent Secretaries they came very near to being accepted. Legislation seemed likely and in November 1975 the Government declared in the Queen's Speech, setting out forthcoming measures for the session:

> Proposals will be prepared to amend the Official Secrets Act and to liberalise the practice relating to official information.

MISC 89 had not reached any conclusions when Harold Wilson resigned as Prime Minister in April 1976 and was replaced by Jim Callaghan.

James Callaghan and the Freedom of Information

Callaghan's views on the Official Secrets Act were already well known. He had told the Franks Committee in 1972: 'I would be inclined to leave it alone as it is ... I see no reason why one should alter things for the sake of it.' But pressure was building up from outside. A leak to *New Society* magazine via Frank Field, Director of Child Poverty Action Group, about the Cabinet discussion on child benefits caused a major political row. A leak investigation was started. The people involved had their fingerprints taken but the source of the leak was not traced. The only concrete result was that Cabinet documents were now stamped to identify which copies had gone to what Whitehall departments, with the aim of making tracing easier in the future.

Inside Whitehall the climate of debate – or the perception of the threat – had changed. If Section 2 was not acting as a deterrent then it was time to introduce modern, effective provisions that could be used. A new Cabinet committee (GEN 29) was set up to prepare proposals. In September 1976 Roy Jenkins resigned as Home Secretary and left the Government to become President of the European Commission. He was replaced by Merlyn Rees.

The new policy was to separate reforms of Section 2 from the introduction of a Freedom of Information measure. At the start of the new session on 22 November Merlyn Rees outlined the Government's thinking on reform of Section 2:

I will, with permission, Mr Speaker, make a statement on the Government's intentions on the reform of Section 2 of the Official Secrets Act 1911. This section, which makes it a criminal offence to disclose official information without authority, has for some time been regarded as too broad in its scope. It has been described as a 'catch all' and there has been uncertainty about its interpretation and enforcement.

The Government have concluded that this section should be replaced by an Official Information Act on the broad lines recommended by the Franks Committee. The Committee, whose membership included representatives of Parliament – including myself – and the media, and which presented a unanimous report, recommended that the sanctions of the criminal law should be strictly limited in their application.

Work was then underway in Whitehall on producing a White Paper to set out the Government's specific proposals on reform.

If there was to be some progress on this front there was to be little or none on Freedom of Information. Callaghan decided not to implement the manifesto commitment. Instead Ministerial reluctance and Civil Service hostility produced a 'compromise' – there was to be no 'right to know' but the Government would, when it thought it advisable, make more information available. Callaghan outlined the new plans in the Debate on the Address on 24 November:

> When the Government make major policy studies, it will be our policy in future to publish as much as possible of the factual and analytical material which is used as the background to these studies. This will include material used in the programme analysis reviews, unless – and I must make the condition – there is some good reason, of which I fear we must be the judge, to the contrary.
>
> I am trying to help. I assure the House that we shall not endeavour to pull back the information. We shall look at every case to see whether we can make it available. The cost to public funds is a factor here, and we should like to keep that cost to a minimum. Therefore, arrangements will not be of a luxurious nature, but we shall make available what information we can to provide a basis for better informed public debate and analysis of ministerial policy conclusions.

The Croham Directive

The strength of commitment by Whitehall to the new approach can be judged from the fact that it took seven months before any instructions about the new policy were issued to Government departments. Finally on 6 July 1977 Sir Douglas Allen, Head of the Home Civil Service, sent a letter to all other Permanent Secretaries. The Croham Directive (as it became known after Douglas Allen, later Lord Croham) illustrates perfectly the failings of the Civil

Service and the true attitude of Whitehall to freedom of information:

Dear Head of Department,
DISCLOSURE OF OFFICIAL INFORMATION
1. During the Debate on the Address on 24 November last, the Prime Minister announced that it would be the Government's policy in future to publish as much as possible of the factual and analytical material used as the background to major policy studies. A copy of the relevant part of the Prime Minister's speech is attached. I am writing in terms which the Prime Minister has specifically approved to let you know how his statement affects present practice and to ask you to ensure that your Department gives effect to it. You may wish to let your Minister see this guidance, drawing particular attention to paragraph 10.

2. The change may seem simply to be one of degree and of timing. But it is intented to mark a real change of policy, even if the initial step is modest. In the past it has normally been assumed that background material relating to policy studies and reports would not be published unless the responsible Minister or Ministers decided otherwise. Henceforth the working assumption should be that such material will be published unless they decide it should not be. There is, of course, no intention to publish material which correctly bears a current security classification or privacy marking; at the same time, care should be taken to ensure that the publication of unclassified material is not frustrated by including it in documents that also contain classified material.

3. In effect, what is proposed is an increase in the already considerable amount of material put out by Departments. The additional material will mainly consist of deliberate presentations in the later stages of discussion and development of new policy. Some of

these will probably, as now, take the form of Green Papers. Some may have kindred form, like the recent Orange Paper on Transport. While most material will be released on the initiative of the Department, probably through HMSO, some of lesser importance, or of interest to a limited audience, may well be put out through other means such as publication in magazines or in response to specific requests in the same way that a good deal of unpublished material is already made available to bona fide researchers. In some cases it may be preferable simply to publicise the existence of certain material which would be made available to anyone who asked. Consideration should also be given to the issue of bibliographies or digests so that interested parties are advised what material is available.

4. In adopting the working assumption described in paragraph 2 above for policy studies, including PARs, (Policy Analysis Reviews) the normal aim will be to publicise as much as possible of the background material subject to Ministerial decision once they have seen the study and reached their conclusions on it. When Ministers decide what announcement they wish to make, therefore, they will also wish to consider whether and in what form the factual and analytical material may be published, since there may, as the Prime Minister made clear in his statement, be circumstances in which Ministers will not wish to disclose such material.

5. It is not the intention to depart from the present practice of not disclosing PARs nor identifying them publicly; any question of releasing PAR material in circumstances not covered by a Ministerial decision should be referred to the Treasury.

6. In his November statement the Prime Minister said that it was the Government's wish to keep to a minimum the cost to public funds of the new initiative on disclosure. One inhibition to the publication of background material in the past has been that it has often

been incorporated in submissions to Ministers which could not be published in their entirety. Re-writing material specially for publication is wasteful and expensive in staff time. Therefore when policy studies are being undertaken in future, the background material should as far as possible be written in a form which would permit it to be published separately, with the minimum of alteration, once a Ministerial decision to do so has been taken. It will generally assist Ministers to reach their decisions on publication if they can see an identifiable separate part of the report appropriately written for this purpose.

7. The form and way in which material is released will have to be considered on each occasion. The cost of any extra printing, or publishing, falls under present arrangements on the HMSO Vote, and HMSO is of course affected by the current restrictions on public expenditure in the same way as other Departments. HMSO is also responsible for deciding what prices should be charged for published material. You should ensure that discussions with HMSO are initiated at the earliest possible opportunity on any proposal which will add to expenditure. The following particular considerations should also be borne in mind:

i. Great care should be taken to keep costs to a minimum. If copies are to be run off in advance of demand, the quantity should be carefully and prudently assessed, to avoid waste rather than to offer instant response. (But, of course, there is a counter-vailing need to aim where appropriate for the economics of longer reproduction runs. The right balance here may be difficult and decisions should not be left to too low a level.)

ii. In general, double printing should be avoided, eg: the published form of the material should be the same as that used internally (and the same print).

iii. There should be a charge for all material, at a price set by HMSO for each item, to include all aspects of reproduction and handling, but not of course any of the costs of the primary study itself.

iv. As regards Crown Copyright, attention is drawn to CSD General Notice GEN 75/76 dated 12 August 1975 (and corrigendum of 8 October 1976).

8. The Government's decision on this question is in a form which should not involve substantial additional work but which could all too easily be lost to view. There are many who would have wanted the Government to go much further (on the lines of the formidably burdensome Freedom of Information Act in the USA). Our prospects of being able to avoid such an expensive development here could well depend on whether we can show that the Prime Minister's statement had reality and results. So I ask all of you to keep this question of publicising material well on your check-list of action in any significant areas of policy formulation, even at Divisional level; and to encourage your Ministers to take an interest in the question.

9. Since the Prime Minister may well be asked what effect his announcement has had on the amount of information made available, I should be grateful if you could arrange to have some kind of record kept of the relevant items made available by your Department. Where material is of an unusual kind, or of a variety not usually made available in the past, it would be useful if a copy could be sent to CSD. In cases where it has been decided not to publish material which might be expected to be of considerable public interest, I suggest that the reasons should be briefly recorded.

10. The greater publicising of material can hardly fail to add to one cost – that of responding to the additional direct correspondence to which it may well give rise. In a Service operating under tight resource constraints, it may not always be possible to afford to give to such additional correspondence the kind of full and studied replies to which we have long been accustomed within

the sort of timescale that has hitherto been customary. Nevertheless, Departments must do their best in these matters, and should inform a correspondent if the timescale for a reply is likely to be longer than normal.

11. I am copying this to Heads of Departments as on the attached list.

Yours sincerely
Douglas Allen

The first point about this letter is that it was an internal document and it only became publicly available when it was leaked to the Press. The second point is that an old Whitehall hand would instantly recognise the tepid enthusiasm behind the letter. Every conceivable objection was listed (including arcane subjects such as Crown Copyright) and every qualification set out. Even the central point was written so as to show how little was actually being changed: 'It is intended to mark a real change of policy, even if the initial step is modest.' An assumption in favour of publication would be made, but the whole process of deciding what was to be published would remain unaltered and Ministers would still decide how much they wanted to release. Even then no classified material would be published. If even Sir Douglas Allen's letter could not be published then clearly not much was going to escape the net. But what was the 'factual and analytical' material that would be published? This was not defined and since in practice such material was rarely isolated from policy advice little would be achieved by the new regime. A large part of the letter was devoted to costs and the importance of keeping these to a minimum. All the emphasis on freedom of information was that it represented 'an expensive development' which had to be avoided if possible.

This letter provides a classic illustration of how Whitehall deals with a problem. The hidden consensus behind the elegant drafting is that the current system is satisfactory but that a small change has to be made to avoid something worse – public access to information. The mystique of policy formulation is to remain closed but some facts might, if the Government thinks they are acceptable, be published. Recipients of the letter would share the hidden views of the authors that freedom of information would be damaging – '*Our* prospects of being able to avoid such an expensive development'. The letter proposes a new policy, but only in general terms, and all the problems are set out fully. Nothing is suggested that will actually change the way in which the machine operates. Also the letter illustrates another classic Whitehall response: there are no instructions in it. This purports to be a major policy initiative but the only words used are 'assumption', 'guidance', 'you may wish to consider', 'should as far as possible', 'I should be grateful if', 'it would be useful if'. Even when guidance is given the letter is very careful to put both sides of the question so that no real recommendation is made. Paragraph 7(i) is a clear example of this and is full of mandarin expressions – 'carefully and prudently assessed', 'to aim where appropriate', 'the right balance', 'decisions should not be left at too low a level'. In the end the paragraph gives no help at all on what to do.

Implementing the Croham Directive

What happened in Whitehall? I remember the letter being circulated around the Ministry of Defence. We were all asked to think about implementing it but no concrete changes were made to ensure that it was carried out. We were simply to 'bear it in mind'. The inevitable happened. The release of information became part of the public relations machine. In one or two cases when important decisions were taken it was decided to issue a glossy brochure giving some extra details but each document was always specially written for the purpose. The glossy brochures were expensive, and they were no more than special press releases to back up the decision already taken: they had nothing to do with genuine freedom of information.

Two incidents a year after the new policy was started in Whitehall make it possible to judge the effectiveness of the new arrangements. In 1976 the House of Commons

Expenditure Committee conducted an investigation into the Civil Service under the chairmanship of Michael English. The Committee's report was highly critical. The Civil Service Department prepared the Government's response. Peter Hennessy, the highly respected Whitehall correspondent of *The Times*, asked to see the background papers. He was told there were no background papers. In July 1978 the Government finally published a White Paper on the reform of the Official Secrets Act. Again Hennessy asked, under the terms of Sir Douglas Allen's letter, to see the background papers. Again he was told that there were none. Callaghan's 'new policy' was a farce. No White Paper is prepared without background papers. Whitehall had obviously decided that all the background papers were policy advice and therefore not releasable under the terms of the Allen letter. Voluntary disclosure it was already clear could not get anywhere.

The Conservatives in Opposition

Meanwhile what progress was being made on reform of the Official Secrets Act? Three years after Labour came into power with a manifesto commitment to reform and the necessary investigation already carried out by the Franks Committee nothing had happened. Legislation had been promised but nothing had appeared. Once again the Queen's Speech on 3 November 1977 promised to change the law:

> Legislative proposals will be brought forward for the reform of Section 2 of the Official Secrets Act.

By June 1978 the Opposition decided to intervene. They secured a debate on 15 June and set about flaying the Government for its failure to act. Leon Brittan, now Home Secretary, was particularly forthright in his criticism of the Civil Service's role in blocking progress:

> In other words, that Section of the Act is simply indefensible, yet it is still there. Why is that? It is still there, in spite of the Government's assurances, because they have not had the courage to fight and overcome the

strenuous rearguard action mounted in the more obscurantist corners of Whitehall. That is the real explanation.

Brave words are always easier in Opposition as the Conservatives' record was to show when they returned to power the next year. Nevertheless the position of the Opposition was made clear – as Leon Brittan said:

It would be very hard to find today any friends of Section 2 of the Official Secrets Act...

The consensus that Section 2 should be changed is based upon a view that it is far too wide in its ambit, covering as it does the whole of the operations of government, and far too broad in the unlimited discretion that it confers on officials to decide what to disclose and what disclosures to authorise. So broad a discretion is barely consistent with any proper concept of the rule of law, which is entirely dependent on certainty of application and the most limited nature of any discretion that must exist.

The main attack came from the shadow Attorney-General, Sir Michael Havers. He commented on the criticisms by the Franks Committee on the 'catch-all' provisions of Section 2:

The stock answer to the criticism which is well set out in that paragraph in the report is that no prosecution can take place without the leave of the Attorney-General and that he will prosecute only where important breaches have occurred. That is right, but it still leaves a measure of uncertainty. In our view, any criminal statute should be certain. For example, journalists are entitled to know where they stand. It is not enough to say, 'All right, technically you will be committing a criminal offence but you are most unlikely to be prosecuted'.

He then went on to set out how the criminal law should apply in future:

The area where secrecy and confidentiality should be

protected must clearly be defined and limited to the extent where it is generally acceptable and compatible with open government. A balance must be struck where the public interest is protected in both ways. I mean by that that the public interest requires that matters of defence, international security and Cabinet minutes, to take just a few examples, may need to be safeguarded against public disclosure. *But the public interest also requires that there is no misuse of secrecy to cover up errors or bungling or to avoid criticism.* [Italics added.]

He set out the position of the Opposition:

We think, as we always have thought, that the Franks Committee was in general right. We accept that Section 2 of the Act is outdated and far too widely drawn. [Italics added.]

He then went on to say that the Opposition wished to go further than Franks had suggested. Under the proposals made by Franks, Ministers would judge the appropriateness of the classification of a document. Havers made it clear that this was not acceptable and that the classification of a document should be decided independently by a Committee of two Privy Councillors presided over by a Lord of Appeal.

Sir Michael Havers had set out the case against Section 2 in a clear and unequivocal way and he had similarly stated the position of the Conservative party in favour of substantial reform. Once in office he was to act differently. Section 2 was revitalised and used with its full power whenever possible. Sarah Tisdall was prosecuted and then he decided to prosecute me despite his statement in that same debate in 1978 that 'the public interest also requires that there is no misuse of secrecy to cover up errors or bungling or to avoid criticism'.

The Freud Bill

Under pressure the Labour Government produced in July 1978, four years after taking office, a White Paper on reform of Section 2. They broadly accepted the Franks recommendations. On Freedom of Information they were more dismissive and finally rejected the 1974 manifesto commitment. The White Paper claimed that following Sir Douglas Allen's letter more official information was being published, although outside observers did not believe the evidence supported this conclusion. The section dealing with the problems of providing a statutory right of access to information said:

> Legislation on these lines would completely change the nature of the Government's obligations: instead of accepting a declared obligation to make more information available, operating on a voluntary and discretionary basis, the Government would be under a statutory duty to disclose all and any information that might be demanded unless it was specifically exempted from doing so . . . This is a matter on which the Government has come to no conclusion and has an open mind. The Government recognises that its proposals do not go as far as the Labour party manifesto of October 1974.

By the autumn of 1978 even the remaining commitment to legislate on Section 2 was beginning to look thin. The Queen's Speech said:

> It remains My Government's intention to replace Section 2 of the Official Secrets Act 1911 with a measure better suited to present-day conditions. My Government will continue to make information on public policy more readily available.

But events were threatening to move out of the Government's control. Liberal MP Clement Freud won a place on the Private Members' Ballot and decided to introduce a Bill to reform Section 2 and introduce Freedom of Information. The proposals had been developed by the Outer Circle Policy Unit under James Cornford and the Bill, with all-party support, seemed to stand a chance of success. Even Jim Callaghan gave it a typically lukewarm endorsement.

It may not discourage the hon. Member for Isle of Ely (Mr Freud) to know that the Government have it in mind not to oppose his Bill on Second Reading.

The second reading was on 19 January 1979. Freud started with an attack on the inability of the Government to implement its own election promises. His scathing attack on the Official Secrets Act highlighted what it means in practice for the individual:

If one wants to find out how to look after one's children in a nuclear emergency, one cannot because it is an official secret; if one wants to know what noxious gases are being emitted from a factory chimney opposite one's house, one cannot because it is an official secret. A man who applies for a job as a gardener at Hampton Court is asked to sign form E74, in case he gives away information about watering begonias. What is worse, if someone is good enough to tell one, then one is an accessory to crime. My contention is that Section 2 gives the Attorney-General more power than a bad man should have or a good man should need.

Freud then went on to explain what the new Bill would do. First it would repeal Section 2 of the Official Secrets Act and replace it with a right of access to official documents but with a detailed schedule of exemptions to this right. The Government gave the proposals limited support and after a short debate, in which most of the contributions were in favour of the new Bill, it was given a second reading.

Over the next few weeks support for the Freud measure grew and the Government hurried out another statement of its view as a defensive measure. It confirmed its view that Section 2 should be replaced, arguing that the 'catch-all effect of Section 2 is no longer right' and that it should be replaced 'by provisions that would restrict criminal sanctions for unauthorised disclosure or communication to a strictly limited range of information'. Simultaneously on Freedom of Information the Government published an enquiry by a team of civil servants from the Civil Service Department on practices elsewhere. Unsurprisingly this group had come to the conclusion that the approach should be one of voluntary disclosure rather than a statutory right to know. The paper nevertheless conceded that something more needed to be done:

> The Government cannot accept that a statutory right of access which could affect adversely and fundamentally the accountability of Ministers to Parliament is the right course to follow. There are other methods of securing more open government which do not carry such damage... Resource constraints as well as experience overseas, suggests that a gradual approach is called for... A code of practice on access to official information, which the Government was fully committed to observe would be a major step forward.

It was the standard minimalist approach long advocated by Whitehall. It represented no real change and there were no proposals for actually introducing a new approach.

The Thatcher Government

These proposals, in the last days of the Labour Government, were never likely to be implemented. There was a general election, the Freud Bill was lost and the Conservatives returned to office with the power to implement the promises they had made, and the brave words they had spoken, in Opposition. In the Queen's Speech on 15 May 1979 the Government promised that:

> A measure will be introduced to replace the provisions of Section 2 of the Official Secrets Act 1911 with provisions appropriate to the present time.

There was no mention of Freedom of Information and it was well known that the new Prime Minister, Margaret Thatcher, was strongly opposed to the whole concept. Nevertheless a Bill was duly introduced in the autumn of 1979 to reform Section 2. An interesting sign of the new attitude was that it was called the 'Protection of Official Information Bill'.

The Bill was first debated in the House of Lords on 5 November 1979 when the main speech was from the Lord Chancellor, Lord Hailsham. He said:

The object of this Bill is to get rid of Section 2 of the Official Secrets Act 1911 and to substitute a code which is more liberal, more intelligible and even capable of enforcement.

He made it clear that the Government accepted Lord Franks' view that the existing Section 2 was too wide and too uncertain in its application and went on to say:

The subject is entitled to know with as much precision as possible what conduct he has to avoid in order not to incur liability to prosecution.

The Government did however go back on their declared intentions, as expressed by Sir Michael Havers when in opposition, that an independent committee should review the classification of documents. A Ministerial certificate was now to be conclusive. And in some respects the Bill went in the opposite direction to the Franks proposals. Official secrecy was to be extended to include the nationalised industries and any mention of telephone tapping and mail interception. Lord Hailsham argued in favour of a second reading for the Bill and did so with a hard-hitting condemnation of Section 2:

Are we to leave on the Statute Book a Section which is really manifestly intolerable because it is unjust and anachronistic; and if tolerable at all, is tolerable only because it is unenforceable and unenforced and therefore brings the law into disrepute? [Italics added]

The Bill attracted much criticism particularly from the Press because of its restrictive attitude to many categories of information such as all matters relating to security and intelligence. As it turned out, it was the latter area that led to the withdrawal of the Bill in the wake of the naming of the Russian spy, Anthony Blunt, in the book *The Climate of Treason* by Andrew Boyle. The new Bill would have made this illegal. The Government withdrew the Bill but offered no alternative and the Whitehall consensus, stiffened by an unsympathetic and secretive administration, left the law unchanged. But the trenchant criticism made by Lord Hailsham still stands with undiminished force.

A further attempt to achieve a Freedom of Information Act came from the back benches in 1981 when the Labour MP Frank Hooley introduced a Private Members' Bill based on the proposals by the Outer Circle Policy Unit that had been the framework for Clement Freud's Bill in 1979. The Government defeated the Bill on second reading.

The subject did not disappear from the political agenda. In 1983 the Labour and Liberal parties included proposals for freedom of information in their manifestos. The SDP was also strongly in favour. At the beginning of 1984 the Freedom of Information Campaign was launched. It received the support of all three opposition parties. It was strongly opposed by the Government. In her reply Mrs Thatcher rolled out the usual Whitehall line that more information was being made available. This, as always, confused information with press releases and propaganda. She went on to make a series of strong points about the relationship between Ministers and Parliament and the effect that freedom of information would have on that relationship.

> Under our constitution, Ministers are accountable to Parliament for the work of their departments, and that includes the provision of information... Ministers' accountability to Parliament would be reduced, and Parliament itself diminished... In our view the right place for Ministers to answer for their decisions in the essentially 'political' area of information is in Parliament.

It was in 1984 that I was to be closely involved in the way in which Ministers provided information and carried out their accountability to Parliament and it was to lead me to the Old Bailey.

PART II

THE *BELGRANO* AFFAIR

CHAPTER THREE

THE SINKING OF THE *BELGRANO*

Anybody who wants to understand the background to the Falklands campaign should consider two important factors.

First, the position of the Royal Navy. The year before the Falklands conflict John Nott had carried out a major review of Defence spending in which I had been heavily involved. The bulk of the reductions had fallen on the Navy and in particular on the surface fleet. The pride of the Navy, the new aircraft carrier *HMS Invincible*, was to be sold to the Australians; the assault landing ships *Fearless* and *Intrepid* were for disposal and the number of destroyers and frigates was to be cut from sixty to at best fifty and of these about fifteen per cent were to be non-operational in the stand-by Squadron. The Navy had never accepted these cuts and fought hard to try and get them reversed. By the end of March 1982 the point of no-return was rapidly approaching when some ships would be sold and others sent for scrap. The Argentinian invasion of the Falkland Islands on 2 April suddenly provided an unrivalled and unexpected opportunity for the Royal Navy to show that it could help the politicians who were in difficulties and thereby save itself. The Royal Navy had one fear: that the Task Force would sail all the way to the South Atlantic and back again without a fight. There had to be a conflict if the Royal Navy was to prove its effectiveness and indispensability. This feeling was allied to the normal military tendency to see any problems in terms of a solution by force of arms. They left it to others to find a peaceful solution if they could.

The second factor was the political position of the Government and in particular the Prime Minister, Mrs

Thatcher. In March 1982 public opinion polls were showing that the Government was spectacularly unpopular; the Social Democratic Party in alliance with the Liberals seemed to be the new political force. Then despite clear indications stretching over many months and subsequently chronicled by the Franks Report the Government lost British territory to a foreign invader – something that had not happened since the Second World War. The Foreign Secretary, Lord Carrington, and his junior Ministers resigned. The Government was in disarray. The immediate response was the despatch of the Task Force, announced by Mrs Thatcher in the historic Saturday debate in the Commons on 3 April. Would it be used or could a diplomatic solution be found? What would such a solution entail? Could the Government survive a diplomatic solution that eventually transferred power to Argentina? Could the Argentinian Government accept anything less? Almost imperceptibly an alliance emerged between the politicians and the Royal Navy. They both needed the other. The Royal Navy wanted to convince the politicians that they could do what was wanted. The politicians wanted them to do it to save the Government.

Article 51 and the Rules of Engagement
The starting point of our narrative is the fact that at no time during the Falklands conflict was Britain at war with Argentina. All military action had to be conducted within Article 51 of the UN Charter which read:

ARTICLE 51
Nothing in the present Charter shall impair the inherent right of individual or collective self-defence if an armed attack occurs against a Member of the United Nations, until the Security Council has taken measures necessary to maintain international peace and security. Measures taken by Members in the exercise of this right of self-defence shall be immediately reported to the Security Council and shall not in any way affect the authority and responsibility of the Security Council under the present Charter to take at any time such action as it deems

necessary in order to maintain or restore international peace and security.

UK military action had to be restricted to that necessary to remove Argentinian forces from the Falklands, and more aggressive actions would have to be ruled out since they would go beyond 'self-defence'. The Foreign Office legal advisers had to be consulted at every stage to ensure that measures being considered would be valid in international law. As the conflict proceeded the Attorney-General, Sir Michael Havers, also became increasingly involved in War Cabinet discussions as legal issues intruded more and more.

The technical term that cropped up continuously throughout the war and in later discussion of the *Belgrano* affair is 'Rules of Engagement'. What are they and why are they so important? Rules of Engagement (ROE) are the means by which control is exercised over naval operations. ROE vary in scope from strategic to detailed tactical instructions. In the Falklands campaign a ROE cell within MOD considered proposals from the Navy for changes in the light of the military and diplomatic situation. The most basic and uncontroversial would be agreed without consulting Ministers. Others would require approval by Ministers in MOD, usually in agreement with the Foreign Office. The most important would need the approval of the War Cabinet. ROE in force are drawn from the standard book of ROE, although this was heavily amended during the conflict to deal with the operational and diplomatic situation. The ROE were not always in line with the public warnings given to Argentina. At times ROE were more restrictive than the warnings because of diplomatic activity. However, the only time when ROE authorised more action than the public warnings was between 2 May and 7 May, as we shall see later in the chapter.

The first British military response to the Argentinian invasion after the despatch of the Task Force came on 7 April. John Nott, winding up an all-day Commons debate, announced the setting up of the Maritime Exclusion Zone, probably timed to coincide with the arrival of the first nuclear submarine in the area:

> From 0400 Greenwich Meantime on Monday 12 April 1982, a Maritime Exclusion Zone will be established around the Falkland Islands. The outer limit of this Zone is a circle of 200 nautical miles radius from Latitude 51 degrees 40 minutes South, 59 degrees 30 minutes West, which is approximately the centre of the Falkland Islands. From the time indicated, any Argentine warships and Argentine naval auxiliaries found within this Zone will be treated as hostile and are liable to be attacked by British forces. This measure is without prejudice to the right of the United Kingdom to take whatever additional measures may be needed in exercise of its right of self-defence, under article 51 of the United Nations Charter.

A fortnight later the first surface elements of the Task Force were sailing south of Ascension Island on the mission that led to the recapture of South Georgia. New ROE were of course required for self-defence of the ships as they entered hostile waters and for the South Georgia operation. 'Self-defence' zones were set up around the Task Force and on 23 April a new public warning was issued to the Argentinian Government:

> In announcing the establishment of a Maritime Exclusion Zone around the Falkland Islands, Her Majesty's Government made it clear that this measure was without prejudice to the right of the United Kingdom to take whatever additional measures may be needed in the exercise of its right of self-defence under Article 51 of the United Nations Charter. In this connection Her Majesty's Government now wishes to make clear that any approach on the part of Argentine warships, including submarines, naval auxiliaries or military aircraft which could amount to a threat to interfere with the mission of British forces in the South Atlantic will encounter the appropriate response. All Argentine aircraft, including civil aircraft engaging in

surveillance of these British forces will be regarded as hostile and are liable to be dealt with accordingly.

That this public warning was issued as part of the South Georgia operation is made clear in the Prime Minister's statement to the House of Commons on 26 April announcing the successful operation:

> I now turn to events on South Georgia yesterday. The first phase of the operation to repossess the island began at first light when the Argentine submarine *Sante Fe* was detected close to British warships that were preparing to land forces on South Georgia.
>
> The United Kingdom had already made it clear to Argentina that any approach on the part of Argentine warships, including submarines, or military aircraft which could amount to a threat to interfere with the mission of British forces would encounter the appropriate response. The *Santa Fe* posed a significant threat to the successful completion of the operation and to British warships and forces launching the landing. Helicopters therefore engaged and disabled the Argentine summarine.

The Government has always claimed that the 23 April warning was the basis in international law for the attack on the *Belgrano* on 2 May. Can this claim be sustained? With a broad reading of the words it is possible to reach such a conclusion, but only on the basis that the words meant, in effect, a declaration that any Argentinian ship or aircraft wherever encountered and in whatever circumstances would be treated as hostile. But it is clear that the British Government did not itself regard the 23 April warning as having such a wide interpretation. Why else did it issue further public warnings on 28 April and 7 May and have a major internal debate about the legitimacy of the warning between 30 April and 1 May? The 23 April warning has been used since the event to justify the sinking of the *Belgrano*; at the time it was obviously viewed as much narrower in scope.

Diplomacy and the drift towards war

Whilst this initial military activity was underway events were moving forward on the diplomatic front as Al Haig, the US Secretary of State, conducted his 'shuttle' diplomacy in Washington, London and Buenos Aires. Could a settlement be put together with American help? It seemed unlikely. While Argentina and Britain might be able to agree about withdrawal of armed forces and interim administrative arrangements, in the end the same question always remained unanswered – who would control the Falklands at the end of the day? General Galtieri could not agree to any settlement that did not at some point ensure that the Islands came under Argentinian control. Mrs Thatcher could not accept any deal that ensured the Islands passing out of British control – it would be unsaleable to Parliament. But the Argentinians knew that any reference in an agreement to the 'wishes' of the Islanders would mean that Britain remained in control. Every peace plan broke down over this fundamental point. Al Haig has described, in his memoirs, the difficulty of the negotiations, moving between the stubbornness of Mrs Thatcher and the incompetence of the Junta in Buenos Aires who seemed incapable of agreeing on any coherent policy for more than an hour at a time.

By late April time was starting to run out for diplomacy as the military imperative began to take over. Elements of the British Task Force were south of Ascension Island and with the southern winter rapidly approaching military action could not be long postponed. Many commentators have speculated about when the British Government gave up hope of a diplomatic settlement. There are, as so often, a number of different versions of events. Lord Lewin, Chief of the Defence Staff, says that the War Cabinet had agreed by 23 April that a diplomatic settlement was unlikely. A message giving this information was passed to HMS Conqueror according to the diary kept by Lieutenant Sethia on board the submarine. John Nott, Secretary of State for Defence, has denied that the War Cabinet took this view and argued that they were actively searching for peace all the time up to and indeed beyond the sinking of the *Belgrano* on 2 May.

Events were now moving towards a climax. On 27 April Al Haig issued his final proposals for a settlement. Haig had always inclined towards the British position and it is highly likely that the War Cabinet were privy to the thinking within the US administration on what would happen if no settlement could be found. As US patience with Argentina was running out, the next move was likely to be for the US to abandon any attempt at mediation and, whilst remaining technically neutral, come out in support of Britain. This was the single most important diplomatic step in the Falklands conflict. US support was vital to keep the Task Force operational, in particular the fuel supplied by the US to Ascension Island. But if the US was to abandon its public stance of neutrality Britain could afford to take a firmer military line without worrying about possible US reactions. Apprised of American views and guessing that Argentina would reject the US proposals, Britain accepted the US proposals. At the same time the Task Force was approaching the Falklands and on 28 April John Nott announced that the existing Maritime Exclusion Zone around the Islands would, from midday London time 30 April, become a Total Exclusion Zone. (This was British Summer Time. Formal times of ministerial statements are in GMT as below.) The arrival of the Task Force gave the UK the power to try and enforce an air blockade of the Islands. The naval blockade was also extended to merchant ships. The text of the announcement by John Nott was:

From 1100 GMT on 30 April 1982, a Total Exclusion Zone will be established around the Falkland Islands. The outer limit of this Zone is the same as for the Maritime Exclusion Zone established on Monday 12 April 1982, namely a circle of 200 nautical miles radius from Latitude 51 degrees 40 minutes South, 59 degrees 30 minutes West. From the time indicated, the Exclusion Zone will apply not only to Argentine warships and Argentine naval auxiliaries but also to any other ship, whether naval or merchant vessel, which is operating in support of the illegal occupation of the Falkland Islands by Argentine forces. The Exclusion Zone will also apply to any aircraft, whether military or civil, which is operating in support of the illegal occupation. Any ship and any aircraft whether military or civil which is found within this Zone without due authority from the MOD in London will be regarded as operating in support of the illegal occupation and will therefore be regarded as hostile and will be liable to be attacked by British Forces.

Also from the time indicated, Port Stanley airport will be closed; and any aircraft on the ground in the Falkland Islands will be regarded as present in support of the illegal occupation and accordingly is liable to attack.

These measures are without prejudice to the right of the UK to take whatever additional measures may be needed in exercise of its right of self-defence, under Article 51 of the UN Charter.

On 29 April the Argentinians replied to the Haig proposals. It was not a rejection, but Haig chose to regard it as such. Negotiations had collapsed. The military imperative was about to take over. What had the Argentinians done to counter the threat to the Islands they had occupied just over three weeks earlier?

The Argentinian surface fleet consisted of the ex-British aircraft carrier *25 De Mayo*, the former US 1930s cruiser *General Belgrano*, two Second World War destroyers – *Hipolito Bouchard* and *Piedra Buena*, two modern Type 42 destroyers bought from the UK – *Hercules* and *Santisima Trinidad*, and three French built corvettes – *Granville*, *Guerrico* and *Drummond*. The Argentinian fleet put to sea between 15 and 17 April and was known as Task Force 79 (TF 79). TF 79 was divided into three groups for operations:

(a) Northern Group: *25 De Mayo, Hercules* and *Santisima Trinidad*

(b) Central Group: *Granville, Guerrico* and *Drummond*

(c) Southern Group: *General Belgrano, Hipolito Bouchard* and *Piedra Buena*

The *General Belgrano* was based at the port of Ushuaia in Tierra del Fuego and left there on her final mission on 26 April. After departure the ship kept close in to the Argentinian coast until 29 April.

The complex train of events that led to the sinking of the *General Belgrano* had started. The events of the next few days have been the subject of much controversy. But since I sent the *Belgrano* papers to Tam Dalyell in July 1984 the British Government has gradually had to admit many of the detailed facts that were first drawn together when I wrote the 'Crown Jewels'. To understand the events we need to look at them in detail, day by day and at times hour by hour.* Before we do so there is one fundamental question to try and decide. Was the British Government, through the GCHQ signals interception establishment at Cheltenham, reading Argentinian signals and was it therefore aware of every move made or planned against them? Early in January 1985 both the *Guardian* and the *Observer* published articles claiming that all Argentinian signals were intercepted, decoded and sent immediately to naval headquarters at Northwood and to Chequers.

FRIDAY 30 APRIL 1982
The British Task Force was nearing the Falkland Islands and at 12.00 the Total Exclusion Zone came into force. When the British War Cabinet (officially known as the Overseas and Defence Committee (South Atlantic) – OD (SA)) met at 14.00 with the Prime Minister, Margaret Thatcher, in the chair and with Frances Pym, John Nott, Willie Whitelaw, Cecil Parkinson, Michael Havers and Admiral Lewin gathered round the table, they faced a clear choice. Was diplomacy at an end and was it now time to unleash the military option? They must have known that Al Haig was

*All times in this narrative are London time, unless otherwise indicated.

about to announce that afternoon the end of his mission of shuttle diplomacy, that the US was coming down on the side of Britain, and that the US would be imposing sanctions on Argentina. They must have felt this gave them much greater freedom of manoeuvre. Diplomacy seemed to be dead. There was no expectation that the Peruvians would suddenly try to revitalise the peace process. They decided to invoke the military option aware of the exposed and vulnerable position of the Task Force as it sailed into hostile waters.

The War Cabinet authorised two major air strikes on Port Stanley airfield the next day. First, a Vulcan bomber, hurriedly converted from its nuclear role to carry conventional bombs, was to fly from Ascension Island in an attempt to close the runway. Second, Harriers from the Task Force were to carry out low level interdiction as a follow-up raid. In addition ships from the Task Force were to provide naval gunfire support.

Then there was a discussion over what to do about the Argentinian aircraft carrier *25 De Mayo* which was somewhere to the north-west of the Exclusion Zone. Aircraft operating from the carrier would significantly increase the threat to the Task Force. The existing Rules of Engagement would allow surface ships to defend themselves, but submarines could only attack ships inside the Exclusion Zone. The War Cabinet decided to allow an attack on the *25 De Mayo* outside the Exclusion Zone and *HMS Splendid* was ordered to find and sink the carrier.

In the South Atlantic the *General Belgrano* and her two destroyer escorts had left Argentinian waters late on the 29 April. Her orders were to steam east on a bearing of 110° for about 250 miles, not to enter the Exclusion Zone, and then return on a westerly course of about 290°. Over the next three days the group of ships was to carry out these orders exactly. On 30 April *HMS Conqueror* was ordered into the area off Tierra del Fuego and told to look for the *Belgrano*. Late that afternoon *HMS Conqueror* picked up the first noises from the group on its sonar – in fact the noisy old tanker accompanying the *Belgrano*. Gradually *HMS Conqueror* began to close in.

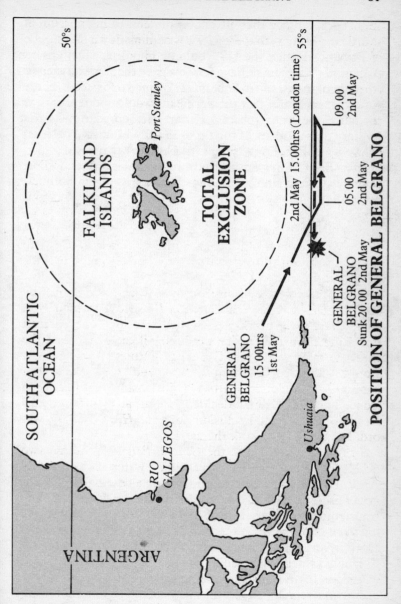

SOUTH ATLANTIC OCEAN

50°S

FALKLAND ISLANDS

Port Stanley

TOTAL EXCLUSION ZONE

55°S

2nd May 15.00hrs (London time)

09.00 2nd May

05.00 2nd May

GENERAL BELGRANO 15.00hrs 1st May

GENERAL BELGRANO Sunk 20.00 2nd May

ARGENTINA

RIO GALLEGOS

Ushuaia

POSITION OF GENERAL BELGRANO

SATURDAY 1 MAY 1982

Early in the morning Francis Pym met his advisers at the official residence of the Foreign Secretary in Carlton Gardens. Michael Havers was also present. They discussed the possible attack on the *25 De Mayo* and the position in international law. It was agreed that Pym would send, on behalf of both himself and Havers, a minute to the Prime Minister and other members of the War Cabinet (Michael Havers was technically not a member), expressing their reservations. The text of the minute was published in the *Observer* on 24 February 1985. It reads:

> Following our decision in OD (SA) yesterday to authorise an attack without warning on the Argentine aircraft carrier outside our Exclusion Zone, I have been giving further thought to the line we should take in public after the event.
>
> After discussing with the Attorney-General the way in which our action would have to be publicly justified and its legality defended, I believe our position would be immeasurably strengthened if we had given a warning to the Argentine Government...
>
> I attach a draft of a possible warning message which we could ask the Swiss to convey urgently to the Argentine Government. This in no way alters the substance of the decision we took yesterday. But I believe it would greatly strengthen our hand in dealing with criticism at home and abroad once an attack on the carrier has been carried out.

Pym signed the minute shortly before he boarded Concorde at Heathrow airport to fly to Washington for discussions with Al Haig.

In the South Atlantic the raids by the Vulcan aircraft and Harriers on Port Stanley airfield were carried out as ordered. There was extensive damage to some of the buildings and a number of Argentinian personnel were killed. But the runway, although damaged, was not closed. Later in the day Royal Navy ships closed in to bombard various installations with their 4.5 inch guns. Britain had stepped up the tempo of the Falklands conflict and the first clear all-out attack had taken place.

Meanwhile, under the South Atlantic, events were also moving fast. *HMS Splendid* could not find the *25 De Mayo* and there was no attack. *HMS Conqueror* was more successful. At 14.00 the first sighting of the *General Belgrano* took place. The elderly cruiser was engaged in refuelling at sea from the old tanker that had been detected the previous day. It was a sitting target but the ROE did not allow it to be attacked. By 15.00 the group were beginning to head off to the south-east, cruising at a leisurely eight knots. This information was signalled back to Fleet headquarters at Northwood where it was immediately acknowledged. It would also have been available to Admiral Sandy Woodward in charge of the Task Force on board *HMS Hermes*.

Later that afternoon the first Argentinian attacks on the Task Force took place. As the British Government have been put under pressure to justify the sinking of the *General Belgrano* these Argentinian attacks on 1 May have grown in size and significance. Newspaper reports and Government communiqués at the time all play them down. There does not seem to have been a major co-ordinated attack pressed home with any determination. The Sea Harriers defending the Task Force were able to maintain superiority. There was only one casualty – a Royal Navy rating slightly grazed by a bullet from another RN ship. But it is clear that after the attacks on Port Stanley the Argentinians expected a major British assault on the Islands. Perhaps this was the long awaited invasion. At 19.55 that evening the Argentinians admit that the Northern and Central groups of TF 79 were ordered on to the attack. This order did not apply to the *General Belgrano* which continued to steam quietly to the south-east keeping well outside the Exclusion Zone.

The British Government have always claimed that there were 'clear indications' of a 'pincer attack' involving the *25 De Mayo* in the north and the *General Belgrano* in the south. But if the British did think there was a 'pincer attack' underway late on 1 May following the attacks on the Task Force did they react accordingly? Commander Wreford-Brown was trailing the *General Belgrano* but he made no request for a change in the Rules of Engagement to enable him to attack the Argentinian cruiser. No request came from Admiral Woodward. At Northwood the Commander-in-Chief, Admiral Sir John Fieldhouse, would have known of the attacks on the Task Force and that *HMS Conqueror* was in a position to sink the *General Belgrano*. He made no move: Mrs Thatcher has admitted that Northwood thought the information about the *General Belgrano* was so unimportant that they did not bother to tell the Chief of the Defence staff, Admiral Lewin. The only plausible explanation is that the Navy did not see the elderly Argentinian ship as a threat.

Late that evening Francis Pym flew into Washington. Almost immediately he gave a press conference. He said that the British attacks of 1 May had been designed 'to concentrate the minds' of the Argentinians in the search for a peaceful solution. He then went on to say that: 'No further military action was envisaged at the moment except to keep the Exclusion Zone secure.' Why did he make such a misleading statement? The day before he had been present when the War Cabinet authorised the sinking of the largest ship in the Argentinian Navy without warning and outside the Exclusion Zone. That same morning he had signed a minute to the Prime Minister, agreed with the Attorney-General, arguing that a public warning ought to be issued before any attack took place. For all Pym knew a British nuclear submarine might already have attacked the carrier outside the Exclusion Zone with massive loss of life. Unless the statement is a complete aberration it can only be seen as part of a public relations exercise by the Government to convince public and world opinion that Britain was using minimum force when in fact all-out attacks had been agreed. What happened next in Washington? Haig claims he met Pym that evening. Pym denies this. Haig says he was working all night with President Belaunde Terry of Peru on the Peruvian peace plan. Pym claims he spent a peaceful night at the British

Embassy and did not communicate with either Haig or London.

SUNDAY 2 MAY 1982

Early on the morning of 2 May (it was still late in the evening of 1 May in Buenos Aires) Gavshon and Rice in their book, *The Sinking of the Belgrano*, say that the Argentinian High Command realised that the British were not about to invade the Falklands. They decided to call off the attack and conserve their ships for a later battle. At 00.07 a signal was sent out rescinding the attack order made five hours earlier. Later at 05.19 the Argentinians say they issued a recall order to the central and northern groups of TF 79. Tam Dalyell has claimed that the order was intercepted at GCHQ and passed to No. 10, Chequers and Fleet headquarters. The *Observer* has reported that Sir Robert Armstrong, the Secretary to the Cabinet, and in charge of all intelligence services and operations, ordered an immediate enquiry early in 1984 when Dalyell made his claim. The *General Belgrano* did not turn round for another four hours. Perhaps the explanation is that since the *General Belgrano* had not been ordered to attack it was not affected by the later orders from Buenos Aires and simply continued on its pre-planned mission to patrol to a certain point and return.

How did the British see the position at this stage? In his lecture to the Royal United Services Institute on 20 October 1982 Admiral Woodward explained how he saw the situation in the South Atlantic:

> Early on the morning of May 2, all the indications were that *25 De Mayo*, the Argentinian aircraft carrier, had slipped past my forward SSN (nuclear submarine) barrier to the north, while the cruiser *General Belgrano* and her escorts were attempting to complete the pincer movement from the south, still outside the Total Exclusion Zone. But *Belgrano* still had *Conqueror* on the trail. My fear was that *Belgrano* would lose the SSN as she ran over the shallow water of the Burdwood Bank,

and that my forward SSN barrier would be evaded down there too. I therefore sought, for the first and only time throughout the campaign, a major change to the Rules of Engagement to enable *Conqueror* to attack *Belgrano* outside the Exclusion Zone.

Woodward's request for a change in the Rules of Engagement was signalled to Northwood early in the morning of 2 May. It seems to have arrived in time to be considered at the regular morning Chiefs of Staff meeting, and in a radio interview on 30 January 1983 Admiral Lewin claimed that he did not know about the request until he arrived at Northwood later in the morning on the way to the War Cabinet meeting at Chequers that afternoon. At Northwood he would have been told two things. First, *HMS Conqueror* had been tailing the *General Belgrano* since 15.00 the previous day, a fact not thought by Fleet headquarters worth passing on before. Second, *HMS Splendid* had not carried out the planned attack on the *25 De Mayo*, indeed contact had never been made.

After discussions with Admiral Fieldhouse, Lewin drove to Chequers for lunch. What happened next has never been disclosed and it may be that only the participants know what really took place. What did Lewin tell the War Cabinet? He probably told them that the planned attack on the *25 De Mayo* had failed – the major unit of the Argentinian fleet had escaped. Woodward says he only asked for authority to sink the *General Belgrano*. The proposition that Lewin put to the War Cabinet was to sink all Argentinian warships on the high seas. No warning was to be issued. In a revealing interview in the *Daily Mirror* on 11 September 1983 Lewin says that he told the War Cabinet: 'Here was an opportunity to knock off a major unit of the Argentinian fleet.' This was to be all-out naval war. It is now claimed that Ministers did not know the position and course of the *General Belgrano*. The orders given were to attack *all* Argentinian ships, so the position of any individual ship was irrelevant. The question that Tam Dalyell, and other critics, has raised is whether the War Cabinet knew of the rescinding and recall orders and issued the order to sink the *General Belgrano* regardless. Did they know anything about the emerging Peruvian peace plan? Did they take account of Francis Pym's minute of 1 May on the position in international law under the UN Charter? Certainly briefing arrangements for such a major decision seem to have been almost non-existent. Perhaps as Lord Lewin has said the War Cabinet was, since 23 April, already committed to a policy of military force.

Several participants have publicly said that the discussion was short, probably no more than twenty minutes. Sir Anthony Acland, Permanent Secretary at the Foreign Office, telephoned Francis Pym in Washington to tell him of the decision. Lewin telephoned Northwood to give the necessary orders. The War Cabinet settled down to lunch before the scheduled meeting in the afternoon.

The change in the Rules of Engagement was signalled from Northwood to *HMS Conqueror* at 13.30. The *General Belgrano* was not sunk for another six and a half hours. Why the delay? The Government say that the original orders to *HMS Conqueror* were garbled in transmission and not clearly understood. But what *is* known is that at 15.00 *HMS Conqueror* signalled Northwood giving the position of the *General Belgrano* at 09.00 and 15.00. This was important information. It showed that the cruiser had reversed course at 09.00 away from the Task Force and back towards the Argentinian mainland. It had kept to its original orders. This westerly course had been maintained for six hours. It is also known that the *General Belgrano* was on a steady course, not zig-zagging and carrying out little if any anti-submarine activity. It is clear that the group was keeping outside the Exclusion Zone and its behaviour suggested that they felt safe outside the area the British had designated as the 'war zone'. Lieutenant Sethia of *HMS Conqueror* has said that it was clear that the *General Belgrano* was not a threat to the Task Force. One possible explanation for the long delay before the sinking is that Commander Wreford-Brown of *HMS Conqueror* did understand the order when it was originally sent. But he did not regard the cruiser as a military threat and so sent back a message giving the reversal of course and the steady sailing of the Argentinian warship away from the Task Force. In effect he was saying 'Do you really want to sink this ship given this new information?' He sat back and waited for reactions.

The 15.00 signal from *HMS Conqueror* was decoded and understood in Northwood by 15.40 and passed to the Ministry of Defence in London. What happened next? Nothing. The naval staff at both Northwood and London obviously felt that Wreford-Brown's information was only of technical value. Why? The Royal Navy had just been given the political authority for an all-out attack on the Argentinian Navy – the exact course of the *General Belgrano* was no longer of any importance. They did not tell Ministers. Admiral Lewin had just got them the authority they had wanted for the last three weeks. They could now show the politicians what the Navy could do. They were hardly going to risk having the whole show called off at the last moment. Mrs Thatcher and the rest of the War Cabinet had been quite happy to give them a complete free hand to take whatever military action they wanted.

The order to *HMS Conqueror* was repeated. Meanwhile the *General Belgrano* continued to sail steadily away from the Task Force. Events on board *HMS Conqueror* can best be described through the eyes of Lieutenant Sethia who was in the control room throughout this period. His diary entry for 2 May 1982 reprinted in the *Observer* on 25 November 1984, reads:

This afternoon I knew what fear was. At 1400 [18.00 London time] we received a signal authorising us to sink the cruiser *Belgrano*, even though it was outside our Exclusion Zone. We had been trailing her for more than twenty-five hours and held her visually at PO [periscope observation].

After tracking her for awhile, we went to action stations around 1500 [19.00 London time] and shut off for attack. The tension in the control room was mounting steadily. We went deep and opened [moved away] from the cruiser's port side to about 4000 yards. She was flanked by two destroyers.

At about 1600 [20.00 London time] we fired three Mk8 torpedoes at the *Belgrano*. The atmosphere was electric as the seconds ticked away: forty-three seconds after discharge we heard the first explosion, followed by two more – three hits from three weapons. The control room was in an uproar, thirty people shouting and cheering.

The captain, at the attack periscope, was screaming out orders – 10 down, starboard 30, half ahead, 130 revs. Everyone was hysterical, stamping and cheering, and it became quiet only after two or three minutes.

We went deep. Then, after about five minutes, there was a loud bang – a depth charge. Everyone froze, but the skipper ordered shut off for counter attack and we took evasive measures, hurtling down to [deleted] feet.

There was silence throughout the boat – suddenly it was no longer fun to be doing what we were. We were at the receiving end.

The message sent by *HMS Conqueror* reporting the attack gave the position and course of the *General Belgrano* at the time but implied that only two torpedoes (those that hit the *General Belgrano*) had been fired. By late on the evening of 2 May the successful operation was known at Northwood and in London, and presumably at Chequers.

What had been happening in Washington and Lima during this crucial period? Pym and Haig had met in the morning, Washington time (early afternoon in London), and discussed the possible Peruvian peace plan. Haig claims they discussed details and individual words. Pym says it was more general. They met again over lunch. Pym says he sent no signal or message to London. In Lima President Belaunde was also working hard. William Wallace, the British Ambassador to Peru, says he was not consulted until early evening Lima time and after the sinking of the *General Belgrano*. The Peruvians and Haig say that he was kept closely in touch. Not much normally happens in Lima. Suddenly it was the focus of diplomatic activity. Did the British Ambassador play no part, or more important send no telegrams to London? The British Government insist he did nothing. Similarly Pym says he only agreed to think about the proposals passed on by Haig and take them back to London. He flew off to New York leaving Sir Nicholas Henderson, the British Ambassador, to talk to Haig. The British Government insist that the 'first indications' of the possible Peruvian peace proposals reached London at 23.15 from Washington and from Lima at 02.00 London time on 3 May.

MONDAY 3 MAY 1982

News of the attack on the *Belgrano* was available in time for the late editions of the morning papers. It was a Bank Holiday in London and the successful attack was reported to the War Cabinet by Admiral Lewin. Exactly how much information he gave them is not clear. The Prime Minister has since denied that she was told about the reversal of course and the position of the cruiser when attacked. Lewin has said he probably did tell them during his briefing. In the South Atlantic, according to Lieutenant Sethia's diary, *HMS Conqueror* had still to worry about possible attack by Argentinian submarines and was forced to dive deep by Neptune maritime patrol aircraft.

HMS Conqueror began, late that evening, to edge back towards the point at which the *General Belgrano* had been attacked with the intention of having a go at the two escorting destroyers. Under the ROE agreed by Ministers the previous day which authorised attacks on all Argentinian warships *HMS Conqueror* was fully entitled to take such action. The Peruvian peace plan was – on the Government's own admission – well known in London on 3 May but no attempt seems to have been made to stop these attacks.

TUESDAY 4 MAY 1982

HMS Conqueror got back to the point where the *General Belgrano* had been sunk but found no sign of any other ships.

Later in the day the Commander-in-Chief, Admiral Fieldhouse, issued orders that ships engaged in rescuing survivors were not to be attacked. In mid-morning *HMS Conqueror* finally found out that it had sunk the *General Belgrano*.

Just after 4 pm John Nott rose in the House of Commons to announce the attack. I will discuss that statement in detail in the next chapter. In the South Atlantic Argentinian aircraft had carried out an attack with Exocet missiles on *HMS Sheffield* which was set on fire and later had to be abandoned. Later in the evening John Nott returned to the House to give the bad news.

5 MAY – 8 MAY 1982

Inside the Government the debate about the Peruvian peace plan and the UK's public position was resumed with the return of Francis Pym from the United States. At the end of the discussion Francis Pym and Michael Havers seemed to have at last obtained the public warning for which they had argued so strongly on 30 April and 1 May. The War Cabinet must have come to the conclusion that the 23 April warning was not sufficient. On 7 May a further warning was sent to the Argentinian Government. It read:

> The Foreign and Commonwealth Secretary made clear in his statement in the House of Commons this morning that Her Majesty's Government's highest priority is to achieve an early negotiated settlement of the current crisis: but that if the Government of Argentina did not show the same readiness and desire to reach a peaceful settlement, it should be in no doubt that Her Majesty's Government would do whatever may be necessary to end the unlawful Argentine occupation of the Falkland Islands. In this context, Her Majesty's Government wishes to recall that on 23 April it informed the Government of Argentina that any approach on the part of Argentine warships, submarines, naval auxiliaries or military aircraft which could amount to a threat to interfere with the mission of British forces in the South

Atlantic would encounter the appropriate response. In addition, all Argentine aircraft, including civil aircraft, engaging in surveillance of these British forces, would be regarded as hostile and were liable to be dealt with accordingly.

In addition, Her Majesty's Government has made clear that all Argentine vessels, including merchant vessels, or fishing vessels, apparently engaging in surveillance of or intelligence gathering activities against British forces in the South Atlantic would also be regarded as hostile and were liable to be dealt with accordingly.

From 1100 GMT on 30 April Her Majesty's Government established a Total Exclusion Zone around the Falkland Islands. Her Majesty's Government will continue to enforce this Exclusion Zone which applies not only to Argentine warships and Argentine naval auxiliaries but also to any other ships, including merchant and fishing vessels which are operating in support of the illegal occupation of the Falkland Islands by Argentine forces; and this also applies to any aircraft, whether military or civil, which is operating in support of that illegal occupation.

Her Majesty's Government has consistently made clear that the United Kingdom has the right to take whatever additional measures may be needed in exercise of its inherent right of self-defence under Article 51 of the United Nations Charter. Her Majesty's Government will take all necessary measures in the South Atlantic in the self-defence of British ships and aircraft engaged in operations and in re-supplying and re-inforcing British forces in the South Atlantic. Because of the proximity of Argentine bases and the distances that hostile forces can cover undetected, particularly at night and in bad weather, Her Majesty's Government warns that any Argentine warship or military aircraft which are found more than twelve nautical miles from the

Argentine coast will be regarded as hostile and are liable to be dealt with accordingly.

The next day, 8 May, the text of the warning was sent by the British Ambassador to the United Nations, Sir Anthony Parsons, to the Secretary-General and other members of the Security Council. The text of that letter was:

I have the honour to transmit to Your Excellency with this letter the text of an announcement on 7 May 1982 by the British Ministry of Defence and transmitted to the Government of Argentina.

The main purpose of this announcement was to reduce the possibility of misunderstanding about the United Kingdom's intentions with regard to measures in exercise of the right of self-defence recognised by Article 51 of the Charter in the face of Argentina's continued illegal use of force to occupy the Falkland Islands contrary to the terms of the Charter and the Security Council's demand five weeks ago in resolution 502 for the immediate withdrawal of all Argentine forces. The announcement also has the purpose of ensuring that the warnings previously conveyed to the Government of Argentina and set out in Mr Whyte's letter of 9 April 1982 (S/14963), and my letters of 24 April (S/14997), 28 April (S/15006) and 30 April (S/15016) remain in force. Finally the announcement gives further precision to the circumstances in which Argentine forces will be regarded as constituting a threat to interfere with the mission of British forces in the South Atlantic, having regard to the continued illegal occupation of the Falkland Islands and the attempted subjugation of the Falkland Islanders, a people of British descent and nationality living on British territory and entitled to the full protection of the UN Charter.

I should be grateful if you would arrange for this letter to be circulated as a document of the Security Council.

Signed   AD Parsons

A copy of this letter and the warning was simultaneously placed in the Library of the House of Commons.

Why is this letter and warning of importance? It shows that the intervention by Francis Pym and Michael Havers on 30 April/1 May was not an academic or legalistic exercise and that there were very real and serious doubts about the adequacy of the general warning of 23 April to cover the circumstances in the South Atlantic. After a debate lasting a week Pym and Havers were able to convince their colleagues in the War Cabinet that something had to be done. The 7 May warning and 8 May letter specifically recognise that the 23 April warning did not give the Argentinian Government clear enough guidance about how the UK would interpret its right of self-defence under Article 51.

Yet for that week the UK Government had been in the position where the agreed rules by which its ships were operating in the South Atlantic went further than the public warnings indicated. And this was the only time that the UK was in such a position during the conflict. On 30 April the War Cabinet had agreed to attack, without warning and without any indication of a specific military threat, the Argentinian aircraft carrier *25 De Mayo* outside the Exclusion Zone. On 2 May the War Cabinet agreed to attack *all* Argentinian warships on the high seas outside the announced Exclusion Zone, again without warning. Under Article 51 of the UN Charter the UK had to report all action taken to exercise the right of self-defence to the Security Council immediately. The actions taken on 30 April and 2 May were not reported for eight days and six days respectively. All other actions under Article 51 had been reported to the Security Council in advance.

The UK Government knew that they were in a weak position under international law for the action they had taken. Politically too the sinking of the *General Belgrano* was controversial and elsewhere in the world British actions were not easily understood. On the 4 May the Government explained what it had done to Parliament. The cover up that lasted for more than two years had started.

CHAPTER FOUR

THE COVER UP

In the previous chapters we looked at what really happened in the South Atlantic in late April and early May 1982. But this was only the beginning of the '*Belgrano* affair'. For another three years the issue remained controversial. It became increasingly apparent that the original explanation of events given to Parliament by the Government was incorrect and often highly misleading. How did the Government get into such a position in the first place, and why did it persist in it so long? The starting point for the explanation has to be the initial statements made by the Ministers early in May 1982.

The Chronology of Deceit

4 MAY 1982

The news of the sinking of the *General Belgrano* reached Northwood and the MOD late in the evening of 2 May and the War Cabinet was briefed the next day at its regular meeting. That day was a Bank Holiday, but John Nott at a press conference said that the Government was committed to a policy of minimum force. (This did not, of course, square very easily with the decision taken secretly on 2 May to sink all Argentinian warships on the high seas.) It was not until the afternoon of Tuesday 4 May that the first statements were made in Parliament. These covered all the events since the previous Ministerial statements on 26 April. The Government thus had at least thirty-six hours to prepare the statements on the *Belgrano*. The first exchange on 4 May came late in Prime Minister's questions. The Leader of the Opposition, Michael Foot, raised the question of the sinking and asked how this could be reconciled with the declaration made by John Nott the day before. The Prime Minister referred to the 23 April warnings and then under further pressure admitted that she knew what John Nott was to say later and saw what the House would hear about:

The very heavy armaments that the cruiser carried, and, of course, the cruiser was accompanied by two destroyers, which were not attacked in any way.

The latter part of this statement was not correct since the accompanying destroyer *Hipolito Bouchard* had been hit by a torpedo from *HMS Conqueror* that failed to explode. The Prime Minister then went on to stress the urgency of the decision that had been taken:

Had we left it any later it would have been too late and I might have had to come to the House with the news that some of our ships had been sunk.

About half an hour later John Nott rose to make the main statement. The part that dealt with the *General Belgrano* was:

The next day, 2 May, at 20.00 London time, one of our submarines detected the Argentine cruiser, *General Belgrano*, escorted by two destroyers. This heavily armed surface attack group was close to the Total Exclusion Zone and was closing on elements of our Task Force, which was only hours away. We knew that the cruiser itself had substantial fire power, provided by fifteen 6 inch guns, with a range of thirteen miles, and Seacat anti-aircraft missiles. Together with its escorting destroyers, which we believe were equipped with Exocet anti-ship missiles with a range of more than twenty miles, the threat to the Task Force was such that the Task Force commander could ignore it only at his peril.

The House will know that the attack by our submarine involved the capital ship only and not its escorting destroyers, so that they should have been able to go to the assistance of the damaged cruiser. We do not know whether they did so, but, in so doing, they would not have been engaged.

This statement contains three major errors of fact:

1. The *General Belgrano* was not detected at 20.00 London time on 2 May. It was detected over forty-eight hours before.
2. The *General Belgrano* was not 'closing on elements of our Task Force'. It had been sailing away, heading for the Argentinian coast for eleven hours before the attack.
3. The attack did involve the escorting destroyers and had they gone back to pick up survivors either later on 2 May or 3 May they could well have been attacked as Ministers had authorised on 2 May since the countermanding orders were not issued by the Commander-in-Chief until 4 May.

In his reply the Deputy Leader of the Opposition, and Shadow Spokesman on Foreign Affairs, Denis Healey, immediately concentrated on the point about minimum force and whether the Government was justified in risking so many lives in a single engagement. John Nott confirmed that it was the Government's policy to use minimum force but refused to say how far away the *General Belgrano* had been from the Task Force when it was attacked. The debate went on but no more substantive points were made except that John Nott strongly rejected a charge from John Gilbert, the Labour MP for Dudley East and ex-Minister of State in the Ministry of Defence, that:

> The attack was not aimed at using the minimum force to achieve maximum military advantage, but that, on the contrary, it was aimed at producing maximum casualties and psychological shock to the Argentines.

As usual John Nott's statement was repeated later in the afternoon in the House of Lords by Lord Trenchard, the Minister of State in the Ministry of Defence. No new points emerged except that Lord Trenchard went even further than John Nott had done in describing the threat posed by the Argentinian ships when he said that:

> There was no doubt about the threat posed by the position and movement of this attack group...

Again this cannot be reconciled with the actual movements of the *General Belgrano* on 2 May.

5 MAY 1982

The next day John Nott had to return to the House of Commons to make a statement about the loss of *HMS Sheffield*. Denis Healey moved the questioning back to the sinking of the *General Belgrano* which suggests he had doubts about what had taken place or at least felt the need for more information. He asked again for the distance between the *General Belgrano* and the Task Force (John Nott again refused to provide it) and went on to say that without this information it could only be assumed that the submarine commander had made the decision to attack without reference to higher authority. In his reply John Nott said:

> I made it clear yesterday that every action by our forces in the South Atlantic is taken within strict political control and authority. The actual decision to launch a torpedo was clearly one taken by the submarine commander, but that decision was taken within very clear rules of engagement that had been settled in London and discussed by the Government. As I made clear yesterday, we regarded the *General Belgrano* as a threat to our forces and we could not conceivably have had any lesser rules of engagement than those which we issued, which were to allow our ships to defend themselves as a fleet.

There are two important points about this reply. First, John Nott seemed to be trying hard to imply that the decision to attack was one taken suddenly and spontaneously by the submarine commander personally, although within general rules laid down by Ministers. In fact, at no time had Commander Wreford-Brown of *HMS Conqueror* asked for authority to sink the *General Belgrano*; he carried out orders given by Ministers, including John Nott. Second, John Nott said: 'We could not conceivably have had any lesser rules of engagement ... which were to allow our ships to defend

themselves as a fleet'. This sweeping statement is at odds with
the decisions taken by Ministers, with John Nott present, on
30 April to sink the Argentinian aircraft carrier outside the
Exclusion Zone without warning and then on 2 May to attack
all Argentinian warships on the high seas.

13 MAY 1982

The sinking of the *General Belgrano* was raised again by Denis
Healey during a general debate about the Falklands
campaign on 13 May. John Nott was winding up the debate
for the Government. Apparently conscious of the need to add
some more information, he said in his speech:

> The *General Belgrano* was in a heavily armed group of
> warships. The cruiser and two destroyers had been
> closing on elements of our Task Force. At the time that
> she was engaged, the *General Belgrano* and a group of
> British warships could have been within striking
> distance of each other in a matter of some five to six
> hours, converging from a distance of some 200 nautical
> miles.
>   Following attacks on our ships the previous day, and
> given the possible presence of an Argentine submarine
> and other information in our possession, there was every
> reason to believe that the *General Belgrano* group was
> manoeuvring to a position from which to attack our
> surface vessels. Therefore, under certain rules of
> engagement that we had already agreed, our submarine
> attacked the cruiser for reasons of self-defence of our
> own fleet.

There are three significant points altogether in this speech.
First, Nott had subtly, but significantly, changed the
wording of his 4 May statement. Now the cruiser and the two
destroyers 'had been closing on elements of our Task Force'
rather than actually closing when they were attacked.
Second, the *General Belgrano* and a group of British warships
'could have been within striking distance of each other in a
matter of some five or six hours converging from a distance of

some 200 nautical miles'. He omitted to point out that for this to happen the *General Belgrano* would have had to completely reverse course. The third significant point came at the end: 'There was every reason to believe that the *General Belgrano* group was manoeuvring to a position from which to attack our surface vessels'. And this despite the fact he had just admitted they were 200 miles apart! What he did not say was that far from 'manoeuvring to a position from which to attack' the *General Belgrano* had been steaming steadily away from any such engagement for eleven hours.

At this point the initial statements came to an end on the immediate circumstances of the sinking. It is worth pausing to try and understand why the Government had made so many incorrect statements, particularly since it is now known that the correct information was available on 2 May. One possible explanation is that they were trying to conceal any prior knowledge of the Peruvian peace plan. This cannot be excluded altogether. Clearly though from the start Ministers were unhappy to take up a public position based on anything other than the use of minimum force and the primacy of diplomacy over military action. The problem was that their decisions at the time on ROE could not be reconciled with this public posture. An all-out naval war had in effect been declared and a decision taken to sink without warning all Argentinian ships on the high seas. This could not be squared with the declared policy of minimum force (and on 4 May when Nott made his first *Belgrano* statement a public warning had still not been issued).

Several features of the circumstances of the sinking of the *General Belgrano* proved to be particularly difficult to reconcile with the public posture. It had been outside the Exclusion Zone and had been sailing steadily away from the Task Force for eleven hours. John Nott seems to have tried to create the impression that the decision to attack had been taken at the last moment by the submarine commander to protect the Task Force. Once they were committed to this version the Government apparently decided to stick by it. It took over two years to unravel the knots they had tied.

Until the autumn of 1982 very little more was heard about the *General Belgrano* in the rejoicing at the end of the war. Then the first books about the conflict were published, among them one by the *Sunday Times* 'Insight' team, a relic of the great investigative team of the 1970s. In the chapter entitled 'Death of the Big Ships' they analysed the sinking of the *General Belgrano* (and *HMS Sheffield*). Three points emerged. First, the crew of *HMS Conqueror* were reported as saying that they detected the three warships of the *Belgrano* group 'at least twenty-four hours' before 16.00 on 2 May. Second, officers of the *General Belgrano* said that the ship had orders not to enter the Exclusion Zone and had been sailing towards the Argentinian mainland when it had been attacked. Third, the book argued that the ship had obviously not been a direct threat when first detected since the decision on whether to attack or not had been referred to the War Cabinet. On 5 October 1982 David Fairhall, the Defence correspondent of the *Guardian*, took up these claims and also gave the first details of the meeting at Chequers at lunch on 2 May.

At about the same time Admiral Woodward was giving a series of lectures on the conflict, including that to the RUSI quoted in the previous chapter. One of these lectures was to Parliamentarians. Among the audience was Tam Dalyell MP. He claims that, although he had opposed the sending of the Task Force, he had not been greatly interested in the sinking of the *General Belgrano* until *HMS Conqueror* returned to its home port of Faslane in July 1982. Commander Chris Wreford-Brown, the Captain of *HMS Conqueror*, had been asked why he had decided to sink the *General Belgrano*. He had replied to the effect that he had not made the decision but had been acting on direct orders from Northwood. This was not the impression that John Nott had attempted to create in his statements to the House of Commons. Tam Dalyell's curiosity was aroused. He wondered what the reason for the inconsistency might be. The lecture by Admiral Woodward and the first reports by the *Sunday Times* team and the *Guardian* clearly aroused more suspicions.

On 29 November 1982 Tam Dalyell had the first answer to what was to prove to be a long series of Parliamentary Questions about the events surrounding the sinking. It was the start of a long, lonely campaign to get at the truth. He was to be opposed every step of the way by the Government who were determined to try and ensure that he did not undermine what they had said earlier in 1982. But Dalyell had a reputation in Whitehall as a great campaigner who once started on a subject did not let go until he was satisfied. The *Belgrano* campaign was to turn out to be one of the longest even by his standards.

29 NOVEMBER 1982
His opening shot, and the answer, was:

General Belgrano

Mr Dalyell asked the Secretary of State for Defence what course the *General Belgrano* was steering when she was torpedoed.

Mr Blaker: The *General Belgrano* was attacked under the terms of our warning on 23 April that any approach by Argentine warships or aircraft which threatened our forces would encounter the appropriate response. There were indications on 2 May that the carrier *25 De Mayo* and her escorts would approach the Task Force from the north, while the *General Belgrano* and her escorts were attempting to complete a pincer movement from the south. Concerned that *HMS Conqueror* might lose the *General Belgrano* as she ran over the shallow water of the Burdwood Bank, the Task Force commander sought and obtained a change in the rules of engagement to allow an attack outside the 200-mile Exclusion Zone but within the general principle set out in our warning of 23 April. Throughout 2 May, the cruiser and her escorts had made many changes of course. At the moment she was torpedoed, about 8 pm London time, *General Belgrano* was on a course of 280 degrees.

Dalyell had obviously been prompted to ask the question following the allegations in the press that the *Belgrano* was steering for home. The answer confirmed that this was the case (280 degrees is just north of west). But there is something strange about this answer which would have been spotted by any seasoned Whitehall watcher. It was long, almost a mini-statement. This is most unusual. Parliamentary Answers are normally as short as possible, giving the minimum information that the Minister reckons he can release. The answer, obviously based on Admiral Woodward's lecture, has an air of attempted justification and says considerably more than it needs to. However, it contains two very misleading statements. First, whilst it was true that Admiral Woodward had sought a change in the ROE to allow an attack on the *Belgrano* outside the Exclusion Zone, the War Cabinet had actually authorised attacks on any Argentinian warships on the high seas. Second, and this misleading statement was to be repeated on numerous occasions over the next eighteen months, the *Belgrano* group did not make 'many changes of course' on 2 May. They made exactly two. One was the reversal of course at 9 am and the other was a minor change from 270 deg. to 280 deg. just before the attack. The wording 'at the moment she was torpedoed' was obviously meant to reinforce this impression and suggest that it was fortuitous that the *Belgrano* just happened to be pointing towards the Argentinian mainland at that particular moment. Yet the Government had given the information Dalyell had asked for and confirmed the westerly course. It is not clear why they did this. Perhaps they thought that if they made one relatively lengthy statement the issue would go away. They were wrong. It only acted as a spur to Dalyell to keep going.

A week later Tam Dalyell established without difficulty the position of the *General Belgrano* when it was sunk. The answer this time could not have been shorter.

DECEMBER 1982

General Belgrano

Mr Dalyell asked the Secretary of State for Defence, pursuant to the reply of 29 November, what was the position of the *General Belgrano* when she was torpedoed.

Mr Blaker: 55 degrees 27 minutes south, 61 degrees 25 minutes west.

He returned to the question of the course. He got this answer, together with a further defensive justification:

Mr Dalyell asked the Secretary of State for Defence, pursuant to the answer of 29 November, Official Report, c. 104, for how long the *General Belgrano* had been on a course of 280 degrees; and what was her immediately preceding course.

Mr Blaker: It is not possible to say: irrespective of the direction in which the ship may have been heading at any one time, she and her escorts represented a threat to the ships of the Task Force, in whose direction they could easily have turned at any moment.

This answer was not correct. It *was* possible to say how long the *General Belgrano* had been on the course of 280 degrees and what the immediately preceding course had been. I had no difficulty in finding this information when the 'Crown Jewels' were written. The latter part of the question is the first realisation that the decision to give the course of the *General Belgrano* had opened a hornet's nest.

A few days later another question produced an even more misleading reply:

General Belgrano

Mr Dalyell asked the Secretary of State for Defence:
(1) pursuant to the reply of 29 November, Official report, c.104 what changes of course were made by the *General Belgrano* on 2 May.

(2) for what period on 2 May the *General Belgrano* was on a course between 010 degrees and 090 degrees.

Mr Blaker: The *General Belgrano* made many changes of course throughout the day. It is not possible to give precise details, but her movements were consistent with the indications that she and her escorts posed a threat to the Task Force.

In every respect that reply is incorrect. The *General Belgrano* did not make many changes of course: she made two. It *is* possible to give precise details and the movements of the ship – sailing away from the Task Force for eleven hours – which was hardly 'consistent with the indications that she and her escorts posed a threat to the Task Force'.

The essence of this reply was repeated by Mrs Thatcher in her reply on 16 December 1982:

Mr Dalyell asked the Prime Minister, pursuant to her answer of 13 December, Official Report, c.11 (1) what was the mean course steered by the *General Belgrano* and her escorts during the time that their presence was known to the Task Force that indicated the convergence of that group with the group of British warships referred to in that answer.

(2) what was the mean course being steered by the group of British warships which would have resulted in their converging with the *General Belgrano* and her escorts.

The Prime Minister: The *General Belgrano* and her escorts had made many changes of course during 2 May. It is not possible to give meaningful mean courses for them or for the British warships. The precise courses being steered at any particular moment were incidental to the indications we possessed of the threat to the Task Force.

The real question asked by Tam Dalyell – how could the *General Belgrano* and the Task Force converge when they were sailing away from each other? – was evaded.

The other problem for the Government at this stage was the Burdwood Bank. Admiral Woodward mentioned in his lecture that he had been concerned that *HMS Conqueror* might lose the *General Belgrano* as the latter ran over the shallow water of the bank. The difficulty was that Tam Dalyell had established that the Burdwood Bank was to the east of the position where the *General Belgrano* was sunk and the ship was sailing westwards! Clearly somebody or something was wrong somewhere.

As Tam Dalyell tried to probe for the facts behind the inconsistent explanations the Government clearly began to worry. It was time to try and stem the flow of information:

Mr Dalyell asked the Secretary of State for Defence, pursuant to the answer of 29 November, Official Report, c. 104, at what time contact with the *General Belgrano* was first made by one of Her Majesty's submarines.

Mr Blaker: It would not be in the public interest to give this information.

The information requested here was released by Commander Wreford-Brown (Captain of *HMS Conqueror*) only five months later (in May 1983 and without his being prosecuted under the Official Secrets Act for doing so). The Government confirmed the information later and it is difficult to see how the 'public interest' has been damaged. If the question had been answered it would have revealed that John Nott had not told the truth on 4 May 1982 when he said that the *General Belgrano* had been detected at 8 pm on 2 May instead of on the afternoon of 30 April. The Government was also just about to repeat this untrue statement.

Another question from Tam Dalyell also got too near the bone for the comfort of the Government:

Mr Dalyell asked the Secretary of State for Defence on how many occasions extensions of the rules of engagement were granted to permit Her Majesty's forces to engage Argentinian forces outside the Total Exclusion Zone or the Maritime Exclusion Zone around

the Falkland Islands; on what dates these were granted;
and for how long in each case.

Mr Wiggin: Rules of engagement for the South
Atlantic were adjusted on a number of occasions as the
situation developed. I am not prepared to give details.

An answer to the question would have revealed the plan to
attack the aircraft carrier *25 De Mayo* on 30 April.
Interestingly there was no claim that the 'public interest'
would be damaged by providing the information.

White Paper, Official Despatch and After

On 14 December 1982 the Government published two
important documents. The first was a White Paper – The
Falklands Campaign: The Lessons (Cmnd 8758). It
contained a narrative of the war and recommendations about
future policy. The second was the more detailed account in
the Official Despatch of the Commander-in-Chief, Admiral
Sir John Fieldhouse, published in the *London Gazette*. Both
these documents contain untrue information. The White
Paper says in paragraph 110:

> On 2 May *HMS Conqueror* detected the Argentine
> cruiser *General Belgrano,* accompanied by two destroy-
> ers sailing near to the Total Exclusion Zone.

The Official Despatch says:

> On 2 May the Argentinian cruiser, the *General Belgrano,*
> with two destroyers, was detected south of the Falklands
> by *HMS Conqueror*.

It is difficult to understand why deliberately untrue
information was published seven months after the end of the
conflict. One of the explanations may be that John Nott was
still Secretary of State for Defence at the time and did not
want to admit that even part of his statement on 4 May had
been incorrect. However, it would have been much wiser, as
Mrs Thatcher finally admitted in the autumn of 1984 when it
was too late, to give a fuller account in December 1982

outlining the main course of events and admitting that it had not been possible to give all the information in May in the middle of the conflict. The general public would surely have accepted such an explanation. But the opportunity was missed and the Government decided to go on trying to cover up what had taken place. A conscious decision was then taken that no more information than the very limited and incorrect versions contained in the White Paper and the Official Despatch would be published, as clearly demonstrated by the new official line on Tam Dalyell's next questions, finally moving to a complete 'brush off':

Mr Dalyell asked the Prime Minister (1) pursuant to her reply of 16 December, for what proportion of the time that the presence of the *General Belgrano* and her escorts was known to the Task Force the Argentine group was steering a course that deviated less than 45 degrees from the bearing at that time of the nearest British ship;

(2) pursuant to her answer of 16 December, what indications unrelated to the course of the *General Belgrano* and her escorts, of the threat to the Task Force, were possessed by Her Majesty's Government;

(3) which was the nearest British surface vessel to the *General Belgrano* at the time she was torpedoed.

The Prime Minister: The official despatch of the Commander-in-Chief of the Task Force has been published. I have nothing further to add to it and to answers to previous questions by the hon. Member on this matter.

Mr Dalyell asked the Secretary of State for Defence (1) what response was received from Argentine armed forces to his communications indicating that the vessels escorting the *General Belgrano* would not be attacked if they returned to the area of the sinking in order to rescue survivors;

(2) how long after (a) the torpedoing of the *General Belgrano* and (b) the time the vessel sank, Argentine

vessels returned to the area; and what were the wind and sea conditions at that time:

(3) for how long the *General Belgrano* remained afloat after being torpedoed;

(4) in what position the *General Belgrano* sank;

(5) where in the *General Belgrano* the torpedoes fired by *HMS Conqueror* struck;

(6) pursuant to his answers of 16 December to questions 116 and 132, if he is able to give the position of the *General Belgrano* when she was first detected by *HMS Conqueror*.

Mr Blaker: The official despatch of the Commander-in-Chief of the Task Force has been published. I have nothing further to add to that and to answers to previous questions by the hon. Member on this matter.

Mr Dalyell asked the Secretary of State for Defence, pursuant to the replies to the hon. Member for West Lothian on 20 December, why Her Majesty's Government have decided to answer no further parliamentary questions on the circumstances of the sinking of the *General Belgrano*.

Mr Blaker: For the reasons explained in the earlier answer.

21 DECEMBER 1982
Immediately before the Christmas recess there was an all-day debate in the Commons on the Falklands White Paper. In a long contribution Tam Dalyell brought together all the inconsistencies in the answers provided by the Government and the inaccuracies compared with the other information he had available. Two members of the crew of *HMS Conqueror*, he told the Commons, had confirmed to him that the *General Belgrano* had been detected long before 2 May. Tam Dalyell went on to say:

In my experience small inaccuracies are often part of larger ones and seemingly small lies are part of larger lies.

He then alleged for the first time the Prime Minister knew about the Peruvian peace plan when the attack on the *General Belgrano* was ordered. It is normal practice in the Commons for the Minister winding up the debate to answer questions raised by members in the debate or to offer to write later giving the information. Dalyell received no reply at all to the points he made in the debate. Obviously it was felt that the less that was said the better and that the issue might go away.

The issue went quiet but it did not go away. Dalyell kept up a low level guerrilla campaign waiting for a favourable break. During January and February 1983 Dalyell asked the Prime Minister three times to set up a formal enquiry into the events surrounding the sinking. The request was refused three times. On 28 February the Prime Minister said: 'There is nothing that can usefully be added to what has already been said.' The matter was taken up, for the first time, in the House of Lords by Lord Hatch of Lusby in their debate on the Falklands White Paper on 17 January. He asked many of the same questions that Tam Dalyell had already raised in the Commons. In winding up the debate for the Government Lord Belstead said that: 'I do not think that to answer that I can do better than repeat the answer to a Parliamentary Question on 30 November by . . . Mr Blaker.' This was the answer to the first question from Dalyell that had already been overtaken by later answers.

At the end of January 1983 Lord Lewin (he had been made a life peer in the New Year's Honours list) gave his first major interview since retiring as Chief of the Defence Staff, to BBC Radio's 'World This Weekend'. Towards the end of the interview the questioning moved on to the sinking of the *General Belgrano*. Lewin was asked: 'From the time that the *Conqueror* sighted the *Belgrano* to the time that it sank the *Belgrano*, how long did it take?' The reply was: 'A matter of hours. On this occasion the communications worked very quickly.' This was misleading. The actual gap between the first sighting of the Argentinian cruiser and the attack by *HMS Conqueror* was about thirty hours.

The publication of a major history of the war by Simon Jenkins and Max Hastings, *Battle for the Falklands*, did not add much new information, but confirmed that *HMS Conqueror* had sighted the *General Belgrano* and escorts on the afternoon of 1 May and reported the sighting to Northwood. The book was surprisingly scathing of the decision taken on 2 May which it described as 'one of the critical decisions of the confrontation, a dramatic raising of the stakes in the South Atlantic by the Prime Minister'. Jenkins and Hastings argued that it was easy to see why the Royal Navy wanted to attack and said:

> But both then (May 1982) and later, it seemed remarkable how readily Mrs Thatcher's Cabinet assented to a step which caused Britain to inflict the first major loss of life of the Falklands War.

They went on to quote from an article in the autumn 1982 issue of *Foreign Affairs* by Professor Lawrie Freedman, eminent analyst of strategic thinking and Professor of War Studies at Kings College, London. Freedman wrote that the attack on the *General Belgrano* was:

> An important military victory, yet it turned into a political defeat because of the premium that the international community put on the appearance of avoiding escalation. Any military action which is not self-evidently for defensive purposes, even if it is pre-emptive, becomes an outrage.

24 MARCH 1983
Meanwhile Tam Dalyell was keeping his campaign going. Late in March there was a short debate in the Commons initiated by Tam Dalyell. This ranged wider than the sinking of the *General Belgrano* but on this particular point Dalyell

highlighted the inconsistencies in the explanations given by the Government that were only serving to fuel speculation:

What is the explanation of the statement by the Secretary of State for Defence on 4 and 5 May? It contains a litany of lies. The first was that the *Belgrano* had been sunk under the rules of engagement. No, it was sunk on orders from Northwood.

Secondly, that the *Belgrano* and escorts were converging on units of the Task Force. No, not at all, it was going 'west-north-west'. No units of the Task Force or Task Group were to the west of where the *Belgrano* was sunk.

Thirdly, he said that contact would be lost over the Burdwood Bank. Again, that was false. The shallowest area of the Burdwood Bank is twenty-five fathoms, that is 150 odd feet of water – and the average is ninety fathoms – 540 feet of water. The *Belgrano* was sunk outside the Burdwood Bank going in the other direction by at least fifty nautical miles. That is fifty-nine miles outside any conceivable limit of the Exclusion Zone. So that is not so.

Fourthly, that it was a threat to the Task Force. It was not. We knew that the range of the M38 Exocets, because we were part of the manufacturers, was twenty miles.

Fifthly, the pincer movement involving the carrier, the *25 De Mayo*. No, the carrier and escorts were in port. I assert that American and our intelligence knew that to be so.

Sixthly, the *Conqueror* detected the *Belgrano* on 2 May. That is contained in paragraph 110 of the White Paper. No, it was on 1 May or possibly 30 April. Members of the crew, with whom I have been in contact, say that the *Sunday Times* book and the Jenkins and Hastings book is correct on this crucial point.

One wonders why there is that inaccuracy in the White Paper and in Admiral Fieldhouse's report. Confronted with half a dozen significant and substantial deceptions and one excuse after another that is being produced when the previous excuse has failed, one begins to wonder.

Dalyell went on to assert that Nimrod aircraft operating from Ascension Island were intercepting Argentinian signals and that they knew that the Argentinian fleet had been recalled early on 2 May. The Government reply in the debate came from Jerry Wiggin, one of the junior Ministers in MOD. Most of the speech was a personal attack on Tam Dalyell, although expressed in Parliamentary language:

One of the hon. Gentleman's endearing characteristics – though some of my long-suffering right hon. and hon. Friends might resort to a less kindly epithet – is the way in which, through thick and thin, he manages to pursue his pet theories long past the point at which anyone else would have realised that he might have got hold of the wrong end of the stick.

In conclusion he said:

I hope the hon. Gentleman will be able to accept – much as it might go against the grain – that he is, not for the first time, utterly wrong.

Time was to show that Dalyell was almost entirely right in his allegations and the Government almost entirely wrong in what they were saying.

Events now began to be swept up in the approaching General Election campaign. On 20 April 1983 Lord Hatch raised questions about the timing of the Peruvian peace proposals. On 12 May in the Commons the Prime Minister, in response to questions from Tam Dalyell, said that: 'News of the Peruvian proposals did not reach London until after the attack.' The same day Lord Belstead gave details in response to questions from Lord Hatch that the first news came in a telegram from Washington at 11.15 pm London time on 2 May. More details of events in Lima and Washington came in an article in the *New Statesman* by Paul Foot, who had recently returned from a series of interviews in Peru without substantially changing the picture that considerable diplomatic activity was underway on 1/2 May although the details were still elusive.

At the end of the Parliamentary session Tam Dalyell secured two Adjournment Debates on 12 and 13 May 1983. They both shed more heat than light and the tone of the Government replies by Cranley Onslow, a junior Minister at the Foreign Office, was very abusive. Dalyell repeated the points he made in the debate on 24 March, and quoted above, about the numerous inconsistencies in the Government explanation of events. Cranley Onslow said in a reply that was both intemperate and inaccurate:

> The hon. Gentleman's behaviour in these matters begins to cast grave doubts on his mental stability. He seems to have an obsession or a fixation from which he cannot free himself. He comes back time and again. However often he may be told that he is wrong and shown the facts, another invention creeps into his mind or inflames his imagination or a journalist eggs him on and off he goes again.
>
> The hon. Gentleman can return to the subject as often as he likes, and I dare say that he will, but he will not alter the facts. The facts are as he has been given them.

The facts, of course, were not as they had been given to Tam Dalyell.

Only a few days later the first major blow to the version given out by the Government came when a book compiled by Geoffrey Underwood was published on 19 May under the title *Our Falklands War*. The book consisted of a series of short chapters on various aspects of the campaign following interviews with the participants. The crucial chapter was entitled 'Sink the *Belgrano*' and contained an interview with the captain of *HMS Conqueror*. The important part was:

> 'We were asked to look for and find the *General Belgrano* group,' said Commander Wreford-Brown. 'It was reported to consist of the cruiser and escorts. We located

her on our passive sonar and sighted her visually early on the afternoon of May 1.

'We took up a position astern and followed the *General Belgrano* for over thirty hours. We reported that we were in contact with her. We remained several miles astern and deep below her. We had instructions to attack if she went inside the Total Exclusion Zone.

'I think the ship's company in *Conqueror* felt we were waiting for things to develop. I felt it was bound to escalate.'

Commander Wreford-Brown said that on May 2 he received a signal from the Commander-in-Chief Fleet's headquarters at Northwood which made a change in the rules of engagement and allowed him to attack the Argentinian cruiser outside the TEZ.'

This was highlighted, under the headline 'Submarine Kept 30-Hour Watch On *Belgrano*', by Desmond Wettern, the naval correspondent of the *Daily Telegraph*. Wettern had a well-developed set of contacts throughout the Royal Navy. Commander Wreford-Brown's account directly contradicted the Government's version that the *General Belgrano* had been detected on 2 May. This point was immediately seized on by Paul Foot in an article in the *Daily Mirror* under the headline '*Belgrano* – The Missing Day in May'. It was another ten months before the Government was prepared to admit that Commander Wreford-Brown was right and they were wrong.

Shortly after this revelation Mrs Thatcher was appearing on an election call programme on the BBC TV 'Nationwide' programme. She was asked, in a now famous confrontation, by Mrs Diana Gould why she had given the order to sink the *General Belgrano* even though the warship had been steaming away from the Falklands. Mrs Thatcher replied: 'But it was not sailing away from the Falklands.' That reply was of course completely untrue. When confronted by Mrs Gould with the facts admitted by the Government itself (the westerly course at the time of the attack) Mrs Thatcher would not admit that her answer was untrue. The argument became more heated and ended up with the Prime Minister distinctly rattled for perhaps the only time in the election campaign. This unusual performance did not go unnoticed. Later Neil Kinnock, soon to become Leader of the Opposition, called for a full-scale inquiry into the sinking of the *Belgrano*.

Just before polling day the *Observer* published a story by Andrew Wilson and Arthur Gavshon, based on research undertaken for a book to be published in 1984, *The Sinking of the Belgrano*. Drawing on information from Argentinian sources, the article published details of the orders to the *General Belgrano* and its movements for the first time. The important points were:

As part of this operation, the *Belgrano* with its two destroyer escorts was instructed to keep south of the British Exclusion Zone at all times, to fulfil a support and patrolling role.

On 30 April the US Secretary of State, Alexander Haig, announced an end to American mediation between the Argentine and British Governments. Early next day Britain launched naval and air attacks on Port Stanley. It was not until about eleven hours later, at 15.55 hours on 1 May, that Admiral Lombardo sent a signal to the Argentine Fleet Commander, Rear-Admiral Walter Allara, ordering him to use his two northern groups to find and attack the British Task Force.

But when, at about 18.00 hours, intelligence from the Falklands reported the British ships dispersed and air and sea attacks ended, Admiral Lombardo ordered the Argentine fleet back home.

Rear-Admiral Allara transmitted that order to his fleet units at 20.07 hours on 2 May and set a course of 290 degrees (that is towards west-north-west). Contrary to the version of its movements since given by British Ministers, the Argentines say it subsequently changed course only once – from 290 to 280 degrees. This continued to keep it well outside the Exclusion Zone and pointed directly towards its base at Ushuaia. When torpedoed by the nuclear submarine, *Conqueror*, with the loss of 368 lives, the *General Belgrano* was only a hundred miles from the Argentine coast and had been on a course away from the British Task Force and the Falklands for nine hours. [*This should be eleven hours in fact.*]

It was, throughout, under visual or sonar observation by *Conqueror*, whose captain has testified that he shadowed it for thirty hours.

At her election news conference last Thursday, Mrs Thatcher said the *Belgrano* was about six hours sailing time from the nearest British surface ship, and so posed a real threat to the South Atlantic Task Force. But Captain Bonzo, speaking by telephone from Buenos Aires on Friday gave us a quite different account of his ship's capability, estimating that the nearest British surface unit must have been at least 250 nautical miles away. It would, he said, have taken him at least fourteen hours to cover that distance at the *Belgrano*'s top cruising speed of eighteen knots.

He said that Mrs Thatcher's claim that the *Belgrano* was only six hours from the nearest British surface ship when attacked was 'absolute nonsense'; also he was not zig-zagging. Until told to withdraw, his orders had been to patrol a line of 200 nautical miles extending from Tierra del Fuego (the southern part of the Argentine) eastwards on a bearing of 100/110 degrees and westwards at 280/290 degrees.

28 JUNE 1983

Early in the new Parliamentary session, after the Tory Government's re-election, on 28 June there was the usual debate on the Queen's Speech dealing with Foreign Affairs and Defence. John Morris, the Labour MP for Aberavon and Shadow Attorney-General, took up the issues raised by Tam Dalyell. What he said is worth quoting at length. He started by commenting on the confrontation between Mrs Gould and Mrs Thatcher:

With the help of the Library, I have read most matters of

significance written about the subject, and I noted carefully the reaction of the Prime Minister when questioned on television by Mrs Gould, a lady from Southampton. I have spent portions of my life closely observing the reaction and demeanour of witnesses, and the Prime Minister's response made me very uneasy. It did not satisfy me to hear her repetitive cry that when all is revealed she will be proved right.

John Morris specifically disassociated himself from some of the attacks Tam Dalyell had made on the Prime Minister. But he went on to say:

However, there is evidence of a *prima facie* case against the War Cabinet, except the Foreign Secretary, and the Prime Minister. The Cabinet has collectively, and she has individually, a case to answer.

He then went on to make detailed allegations:

I hope that the House will consider my case for an inquiry on the basis of a series of questions to which I have failed to find a satisfactory answer, or where answers have been contradicted from time to time by later evidence.

John Morris concluded after making fifteen detailed points on all the inconsistencies in the Government's explanations by saying:

I have tried, I hope coolly and clinically, to sift the wheat from the chaff on this issue. I have tried to discover the answers to my own questions. I have tried to reconcile what is apparently irreconcilable. It would be a very serious matter indeed if serious doubt remained that the single act of changing the policy on firing at such a short notice, with extremely limited consultation, resulted in a substantial acceleration of the war and subsequent loss of life on both sides when there were serious hopes that it could have been brought to an end. If that were conclusively proved, it would be a national and personal disgrace. I believe that some doubts have been raised by my hon. Friend the Member for Linlithgow. I have sought to set them out. They will not go away. The highest tribunal is necessary to examine the facts, the state of the deliberations, the intelligence available and, in particular, the log of the *Conqueror*.

Here was a logical and closely argued speech from a trained legal brain and a senior opposition spokesman. Grave allegations were made abut the conduct of the Government both at the time of the Falklands conflict and subsequently. What was the response of the Government? No reply was ever given. Clearly the Government could not answer the questions without some very embarrassing relevations. Bolstered by a substantial Commons majority no doubt they hoped the issue would disappear if treated with studied neglect.

13th JULY 1983

Others were not prepared to accept a refusal to comment. A fortnight later Lord Hatch of Lusby secured a short debate in the Lords. At the start of his speech he went to the heart of the matter, raising the issue of Ministerial accountability to Parliament:

My concern is that a series of contradictory statements appears to have been made by the Government, dubious answers given to questions and hidden evidence. Therefore, there is public concern whether and when the Government are telling the truth.

Lord Hatch went on to put many of the same inconsistencies in replies that had been used by John Morris in his speech in the Commons.

After a few interventions Baroness Young made the Government's reply. It repeated the usual line about knowledge of the Peruvian peace plan and rejected calls for an inquiry. But once again the untrue statement that: 'The cruiser had changed her course many times during the day' was repeated. In addition the misleading statement was made that: 'Ministers approved a change in the rules of engagement, requested by the Task Force Commander, to enable the cruiser to be engaged outside the Total Exclusion Zone'. This again disguised the fact that the real decision taken on 2 May had been to attack all Argentinian warships, not just the *General Belgrano*. But on one point the Government decided that it had to give ground. It could no longer maintain the line that detection of the *General Belgrano* had taken place on 2 May now that the Captain of *HMS Conqueror* was on record as saying it took place on 1 May, if not earlier. A new line was required. Baroness Young said, referring to the statement in the Falklands White Paper published just six months earlier:

> The paragraph in question deals with the question of the events which took place on 2 May last year. It was not intended to indicate when the cruiser was first located.

This was a pathetic attempt to wriggle out of the difficulty and square the circle. The paragraph in question (paragraph 110) is absolutely explicit:

> On 2 May *HMS Conqueror* detected the Argentine cruiser, *General Belgrano* . . .

Nothing could be clearer.

In Parliament there was a temporary lull. But outside a number of events were in train that were to transform the situation and eventually cause considerable panic in the Government and lead to me being asked to write the 'Crown Jewels'. Tam Dalyell visited Lima and gained more evidence about the Peruvian peace plan. On 12 January 1984, Dalyell alleged that the recall signal early on 2 May was decoded and sent immediately to Chequers. In other words he alleged the War Cabinet knew that there was no attack in progress when they ordered the all-out attack on the Argentinian fleet on 2 May.

In addition to these sources, in the autumn of 1983 the diary of Lieutenant Sethia, who was the Supplies Officer of *HMS Conqueror*, became available to both Tam Dalyell and

Arthur Gavshon. This confirmed that the Government's account of events was almost totally inaccurate and must have encouraged them both to go on probing. By then Arthur Gavshon was working, in conjunction with Desmond Rice, on *The Sinking of the Belgrano*. As part of their research they asked to interview Lord Lewin, Admiral Woodward and Commander Wreford-Brown. They were told by the Ministry of Defence that they should approach Lord Lewin direct since he had retired. The request to interview Commander Wreford-Brown was rejected, no doubt because he was too closely involved in the sinking of the *General Belgrano*. An interview with Admiral Woodward was also rejected, no doubt because it would have been almost impossible to ensure that the complex and inconsistent position adopted by the Government was maintained throughout a live interview. Gavshon and Rice were told instead to submit written questions. This they did. In all there were nine questions which showed a good grasp of the weaknesses of the Government's position. Answers to these questions were prepared at the end of 1983 in line with previous Government statements. They were sent to John Stanley, the Minister of State, for clearance. He took about six weeks to consider them and then on 16 January 1984 he rejected them.

The book was published – without Stanley's contribution – early in March 1984. It was the first detailed account of events to be publicly available and it directly contradicted the Government's version in virtually every respect. It contained details of the Peruvian peace proposals and the orders to the Argentinian fleet. It also contained long extracts from the diary kept by Lieutenant Sethia but without attribution and it was not immediately apparent where they had obtained the information. The book sold out on publication and re-opened the controversy.

21 FEBRUARY 1984

Unfortunately for the Government, just before the publication Tam Dalyell had been able to obtain a slot to ask the

Prime Minister at Question Time about the sinking in forthright terms and was driven to use 'unparliamentary language'.

Mr Dalyell asked the Prime Minister why she will not set up a public inquiry into the circumstances surrounding the sinking of the *Belgrano*.

The Prime Minister: The Government have explained very fully and on numerous occasions both in this House and in another place the reasons for the attack on the *General Belgrano*. An inquiry into the affair would therefore serve no useful purpose.

Mr Dalyell: As the captain of the *Conqueror* has said in print that he was following the *General Belgrano* for at least thirty hours and the Government persists in claiming that the *General Belgrano* was detected on the same day as it was sunk, who is telling the truth or, bluntly, is it the submarine commander or the Prime Minister who is lying?

Mr Speaker: Order. The hon. Member must not use that word. I am sure that he will rephrase that final comment.

Mr Dalyell: Is it the submarine commander or the Prime Minister who is telling the truth?

Prime Minister: The full facts were given in several replies in the House... All the facts are there. They support the Government's case.

This exchange is important for two reasons. First, it shows that the Government were still forcefully sticking to the line in public that they had already given a full and truthful account of events. (Yet only six weeks later the Prime Minister was forced to admit that the full facts had not been given in several replies in the House.) Second, the Table Office (which controls the placing of Parliamentary Questions by MPs) argued that this reply now precluded further questions on the *Belgrano* from Tam Dalyell. If the Prime

Minister said that all the facts were available then Parliamentary time could not be wasted by asking further questions. If there had not been other developments that misleading reply from the Prime Minister might successfully have blocked further questioning.

MARCH 1984

Early in March John Stanley answered a question from Tam Dalyell about the refusal to answer the questions from Gavshon and Rice and took the same line as the Prime Minister.

> **Mr Dalyell** asked the Secretary of State for Defence why, on 16 January, his Department refused the request originally made on 26 June 1983 by Desmond Rice and Arthur Gavshon, and Messrs Secker and Warburg to interview Rear Admiral Sir John Woodward and Commander Christopher Wreford-Brown, DSO, Royal Navy, about the sinking of the *General Belgrano*; and if he will make a statement.

> **Mr Stanley:** As my right hon. Friend the Prime Minister said to the hon. Gentleman on 21 February 1984, the circumstances of the sinking of the *General Belgrano* have been set out both in the House and in another place. This request for interviews was accordingly declined.

It was at this point that the Shadow Cabinet took up the issue and Denzil Davies wrote to the Prime Minister on their behalf. This was followed up by a letter from Tam Dalyell to Michael Heseltine. The Gavshon and Rice book had just been published. The issue was re-opened with a vengeance and the Government was under pressure.

In March 1984 the Government's public position was that the facts were:

1. The *General Belgrano* had been detected on 2 May.
2. The impression was given that no decision had been made to attack *25 De Mayo*.

3. Although the *General Belgrano* was on a course of 280 degrees at the time of attack it was a clear threat to the Task Force.
4. The *General Belgrano* made many changes of course on the 2 May.
5. The change in the ROE made at Chequers on 2 May had been limited to allow *HMS Conqueror* to attack the *General Belgrano* outside the Exclusion Zone.
6. The escorting destroyers had not been attacked in any way.

Since March 1984 they have admitted that the position actually was that:

1. The *General Belgrano* and the group of escorting ships were detected by *HMS Conqueror* on 30 April 1982 and first sighted on 1 May 1982.
2. On 30 April 1982 the UK Government decided to attack the aircraft carrier *25 De Mayo* outside the Exclusion Zone and without issuing a warning to the Argentinian Government.
3. The *General Belgrano* reversed course away from the UK Task Force at 09.00 London time on 2 May and continued to sail away for eleven hours before it was attacked.
4. The *General Belgrano* made only two changes of course on 2 May. The reversal of course at 09.00 and one shortly before the attack – a minor change from 270 degrees to 280 degrees.
5. The change in the ROE made at Chequers at lunchtime on 2 May authorised attacks on any Argentinian warship outside Argentinian territorial waters.
6. The two destroyers escorting the *General Belgrano* were attacked on 2 May (either deliberately or possibly accidentally) as the ROE authorised. *HMS Conqueror* returned to the scene on 3 May to continue the attack but was ordered on 4 May to stop.

CHAPTER FIVE

THE BATTLE FOR THE TRUTH

The Making of the 'Crown Jewels'

The 'Crown Jewels' is the 'Top Secret' Ministry of Defence study of the events surrounding the sinking of the *General Belgrano* by *HMS Conqueror* in May 1982 and it is now an open secret that it contains very highly classified intelligence information. I wrote the 'Crown Jewels' in late March 1984 when the Government was under strong political pressure to explain why it had sunk the old Argentinian cruiser. The document itself is a detailed log of every significant event in London and the South Atlantic from 7 April to 7 May 1982.

Early in March 1984 I had become Head of DS5, one of the divisions within MOD responsible for controlling military operations. When I arrived in my tiny, cold and gloomy office on the north side of the huge, grey neo-Stalinist Defence Ministry building in Horse Guards Avenue, there were no less than four telephones on the desk, one for ordinary calls, one an intercom with other members of the naval staff, the other two secure phones for classified conversations. The sense that a crisis or the Third World War might happen at any time was heightened when I was handed the 'bleeper' that I had to carry at all times (on or off duty) just in case the crisis blew up in the lunch-hour.

Most of my time ought to have been dealing with the Iran–Iraq war and the possible conflict in the Gulf. Instead I found that I had to deal with the political consequences of a decision taken two years earlier as the Falklands conflict moved into a real shooting war. The sinking, by *HMS Conqueror*, on 2 May 1982 of the old 1930s ex-US Navy cruiser *General Belgrano* was the most important military action of the conflict, causing the biggest loss of life in any single UK military action since the Second World War. There had been political controversy from the time the sinking was first announced in the House of Commons on 4 May 1982 and the event had been immortalised in the most controversial newspaper headline of the period – 'Gotcha!'

Only a fortnight after taking over as Head of DS5 I was in Michael Heseltine's office on the sixth floor of the MOD building overlooking the Thames talking to one of the two Assistant Private Secretaries about some aspect of the Gulf war, when Richard Mottram, the Private Secretary, told me that he was sending out a minute asking me to do a complete investigation into the sinking of the *Belgrano* on behalf of the Secretary of State. The Shadow Cabinet had taken up the issue in a letter to the Prime Minister and I had been asked by John Stanley, the Minister of State, to produce two draft replies. One would give the correct date of the detection and sighting of the *General Belgrano*, the other would stick to the earlier incorrect version. Ministers wanted to choose which one they would use. Tam Dalyell also sent in a letter asking nine detailed questions. Michael Heseltine had been Secretary of State for Defence for over a year but had not been interested in the *Belgrano* affair before. Now it was a live political issue and he was worried. As Heseltine was heard to say around Westminster, 'I want to be quite sure that there is not a Watergate in this somewhere!' No. 10 had been told that the investigation was to take place. I was asked to produce a detailed chronology of events dealing with all aspects of the sinking, including the possible Peruvian peace plan. This was to be a comprehensive account covering all the information and not just that which had been used to back up the Government's public line until then. Heseltine wanted to make as much of this information public as possible. I had just a week in which to do the work.

This was obviously a frantic period. Records had to be called back from archives; papers from other divisions in MOD had to be located, read and processed; the detailed information held at Fleet Headquarters at Northwood just outside London needed to be analysed; access was required to very highly classified material. Gradually the main events were pieced together in an attempt to understand what had happened. I had easy access to all the Defence archives and records, but was less lucky with the Foreign Office files. They simply sent two telegrams, one from Washington and one from Peru, dated late on the evening of 2 May 1982, giving the 'first indications' about the Peruvian peace plan. I was assured that there were no others. After a flurry of intense activity – writing and typing – the account was ready. It was a document of about twenty-five or thirty pages giving a detailed chronology of every event that seemed to be relevant. It was very highly classified and only six copies were made. After my arrest somebody told Tam Dalyell of the existence of this document, referring to it as the 'Crown Jewels' – a term that I had never heard used in MOD. But the name stuck. When Michael Heseltine gave evidence to the Foreign Affairs Committee in November 1984 even he referred to it as the 'Crown Jewels', and throughout my trial the document was always called that.

Within twenty-four hours of completing the 'Crown Jewels' and discovering both the truth about events in 1982 and the scale of the cover up I had plunged into a remarkable series of meetings with Ministers to decide how the Government should deal with the situation that had been revealed.

The morning of 30 March 1984: the office of the Secretary of State for Defence

The first meeting took place in Michael Heseltine's office. We had to consider how to reply to two letters. The first was from Denzil Davies, the Opposition Defence spokesman, who had written on 6 March to the Prime Minister on behalf of the Shadow Cabinet expressing concern about discrepancies in the various accounts of the sinking. The text of the letter was:

Dear Prime Minister
I am writing on behalf of the Shadow Cabinet to ask for

your comments on the serious discrepancies which exist between the Government's version of the circumstances surrounding the sinking of the *General Belgrano* by *HMS Conqueror* on 2 May 1982 and statements made regarding the affair in two recent publications.

The Government maintains, in paragraph 110 of the Falklands Campaign: the Lessons, Cmnd 8758 that the *Conqueror* detected the *Belgrano* on 2 May 1982. Yet in the book *Our Falklands War: The Men of the Task Force Tell THEIR Story* by Geoffrey Underwood, the Commander of the *Conqueror* is reported to have said that he visually sighted the *Belgrano* early in the afternoon of 1 May and followed it for over thirty hours.

In another book published on 5 March, *The Sinking of the Belgrano* by Desmond Rice and Arthur Gavshon, the authors also maintain that the *General Belgrano* had been located forty-eight hours before it was sunk and was then trailed for more than thirty hours. They further assert that when the *Belgrano* was sunk it was on course for the Argentine coastline.

Because of the widespread concern regarding the reasons behind the sinking of the *Belgrano*, I should be grateful for your comments.

Yours sincerely
The Right Hon. Denzil Davies, MP

This was the first time that the Shadow Cabinet had taken up the *Belgrano* question and clearly the Government could not brush this aside as it had Tam Dalyell for the previous two years. The letter from Denzil Davies might be the start of a process by which the *Belgrano* affair became a major political issue.

The second letter was from Tam Dalyell to Michael Heseltine. This had been sent on 19 March and asked nine detailed questions about the time and detection of the *Belgrano*, its course on 1–2 May and detailed questions about the attack. When I studied the letter it was clear that Dalyell had access to some very accurate information. The Government had never acknowledged the detailed sequence of events over the period 30 April to 2 May 1982, yet Dalyell obviously knew exactly what they were. It is now apparent that the source was the diary kept by Lieutenant Sethia; at the time we could only speculate. Also Dalyell knew a great deal about the *25 De Mayo*; he probably knew about the 30 April decision to attack outside the Exclusion Zone and the real nature of the 2 May decision since both were in the Gavshon and Rice book. All his questions would have to be handled with care.

The meeting with Michael Heseltine started just before 10.00 on 30 March and lasted until nearly 13.00. This was a very long meeting by his standards and a number of other appointments that morning had to be cancelled. By the end there was a long queue of people outside in the private office waiting to see the Secretary of State. The other Minister present was John Stanley, the junior Minister and a former Parliamentary Private Secretary to Margaret Thatcher when she was Leader of the Opposition. A remarkably zealous and loyal acolyte of the Prime Minister, he had once said to me: 'Margaret Thatcher is too good for this country. The country does not deserve somebody so outstanding. She is the greatest leader this country has been privileged to have this century, and that includes Winston Churchill.' The others present that morning were Richard Mottram, Heseltine's Private Secretary; Sir Clive Whitmore, the Permanent Secretary (who had been Private Secretary to Mrs Thatcher during the Falklands campaign, and had decided to attend the meeting once he heard it was about the *Belgrano*); and Admiral Sir John Fieldhouse, the First Sea Lord, who had been Commander-in-Chief at Northwood during the Falklands campaign.

Throughout the meeting Michael Heseltine as usual lounged languidly on his settee with his feet up, idly flipping through the 'Crown Jewels'. The table was covered with coffee cups and laid out on the floor was a large scale map of the South Atlantic on which we tried to plot the movements of the *General Belgrano* and its exact position at the important moments. This task was not made any easier by John Stanley's contributions. As an acknowledged '*Belgrano* bore' he knew the Gavshon and Rice book *Sinking of the Belgrano* backwards and he would keep reading out selected extracts from the book. The problem was that Gavshon and Rice used local South Atlantic time throughout whereas the 'Crown Jewels' used Greenwich Mean Time. As we all tried to convert from one to the other the level of confusion mounted. The discussion was not structured and we went round and round the same points.

Suddenly Admiral Fieldhouse claimed that his official despatch on 14 December had been deliberately altered by Whitehall to put in the false date of detection of the *Belgrano*. This was denied, but we were never able to establish just why this had been done or who had done it. Admiral Fieldhouse left the meeting after an hour in order to fly off to America. A few minutes later John Stanley announced he had to leave to go to a constituency engagement.

'No, I want you to stay, John,' said Heseltine.

'But I've got to get there by twelve o'clock and I've put it off once already,' replied Stanley.

'Oh, don't worry about that, I've put that sort of thing off six or seven times before finally going. This is much more important.'

'No, I'll have to go.'

'Can we get a helicopter to take him down?' Heseltine asked Richard Mottram.

'Sorry we can't do that, it's a party engagement, so he can't use an official helicopter,' was the reply.

'Well, John, go and phone them up and tell them you're going to be very late. I'm not letting you go yet.'

John Stanley shuffled out of the room to phone his constituency secretary. When he came back he did not rejoin the circle around Heseltine's sofa but went to the desk at the back of the room and sulked whilst he leafed through the papers.

I cannot discuss everything that took place at this extraordinary meeting because some of it is very highly classified, but the conversation essentially revolved around the question of whether it was right politically to admit that the Government's line on the time of detection had been wrong for nearly two years. On the one hand it was argued that changing the public position would probably only 'encourage' Dalyell to keep going. On the other hand the alternatives were not very attractive either.

'I think we should claim everything is classified and refuse to answer any of the questions,' said Stanley.

'But none of the information is classified,' I replied. 'And if we try and say that the information is classified what are we going to reply when somebody asks when are we going to prosecute Commander Wreford-Brown under the Official Secrets Act for giving out the information a year ago?' I added. 'That's a good point, John,' said Heseltine. 'After Tisdall [Sarah Tisdall had just been sent to prison for six months under the Official Secrets Act] I can't face another secrets case.'

After much discussion it was finally agreed that it was no longer possible to keep up the pretence that the *General Belgrano* was detected on 2 May 1982 as John Nott had told the House of Commons on 4 May 1982 – a line which the White Paper on 14 December 1982 and the Official Despatch had repeated. We moved on to the questions put by Tam Dalyell in his letter. Without too much difficulty we agreed that if the right time of detection of the *General Belgrano* was finally admitted then the intervening events up to the sinking would also have to be made public. Indeed Denzil Davies was already asking about this aspect of the story. John Stanley tried once again to claim that all of this information was classified and could not be released. I pointed out that it was not classified, that all we would be doing would be providing some detail about a piece of military history, and that the Argentinians presumably already knew where their own ship had been on 1/2 May 1982.

Just before lunch the meeting broke up with general agreement that a new policy of greater openness was to be adopted and that the cover up was essentially at an end. After lunch Sir Clive Whitmore phoned me to say that he and Michael Heseltine were going over to No. 10 that afternoon and would be taking a copy of the 'Crown Jewels' to brief the Prime Minister and get her agreement on handling the information that had been discovered. I heard no more until nearly 7 o'clock that evening. As I arrived home from work, the phone rang; it was one of Heseltine's Private Secretaries asking me to come straight back into the office for another meeting.

The evening of 30 March 1984:
the office of the Secretary of State for Defence

I drove down to the Ministry of Defence building just off Whitehall and arrived in Heseltine's office just before he returned from No. 10 accompanied by Sir Clive Whitmore. Mrs Thatcher had agreed to finally admit the true date of detection and sighting of the *General Belgrano*. But the draft reply to Denzil Davies would have to be worked up further to try and disguise as much as possible the shift of position. I was asked to rephrase the letter, placing the greatest possible emphasis on the Argentinian attacks on 1 May. This proved somewhat difficult because the level of attacks had actually been very low and ineffective. We agreed to meet again on Sunday evening to discuss the drafts. I went off to do the redrafting and about 9 o'clock that same evening I gave the new draft to Sir Clive Whitmore for him to take home and consider on the Saturday.

The afternoon of 1 April 1984:
the office of the Secretary of State for Defence

We all (minus Sir John Fieldhouse) reconvened in Michael Heseltine's office late in the afternoon. John Stanley opened by saying that he wished he had been present at the meeting with the Prime Minister because he would have argued strongly in favour of claiming that all the information was classified and could not therefore be released, even though he had been told that this was not the case. Since the Prime

Minister had made her decision, we carried on working on the revised draft. John Stanley suggested including the passage on the *Belgrano* from Admiral Woodward's lecture. I pointed out that if we introduced this passage we were in danger of implying that the decision taken on 2 May had been limited to allowing *HMS Conqueror* to attack just the *General Belgrano*, whereas the actual decision had been to authorise attacks on all Argentinian ships. Sir Clive Whitmore's view was that we were not telling a direct lie. He argued it was all right to imply this as long as we did not explicitly state it as being correct. After the meeting I again redrafted the letter in accordance with the new set of instructions and left the office to enjoy what remained of the weekend.

The reply to Denzil Davies

The next day (Monday 2 April) I kept in touch with Heseltine's private office and heard that the draft reply had been approved by Heseltine and sent over to No. 10. Apparently Mrs Thatcher was to have a meeting with Willie Whitelaw and the Chief Whip later that morning to discuss the political acceptability of the reply and whether the Government was wise to start changing its story about the sinking. Obviously they must have agreed with the proposed reply for it was sent to Denzil Davies on 4 April. The full text of the reply is:

10 Downing Street

The Prime Minister

4 April 1984

Dear Mr Davies,

Thank you for your letter of 6 March about the sinking of the *General Belgrano*.

The background to this event is worth recalling. On 30 April a Total Exclusion Zone was established around the Falkland Islands. On 1 May attacks by Vulcan and Sea Harrier aircraft were carried out on Stanley airfield as part of the process of enforcing the Total Exclusion Zone. On the same day the Task Force came under attack for the first time from the Argentine airforce and some Argentine aircraft were shot down. We were all very conscious of the risk that these assaults on the Task Force would be backed up by attacks by surface ships and submarines of the Argentine Navy and by aircraft from their carrier, the *25 De Mayo*. All British units were on maximum alert to deal with any naval or air attacks.

HMS Conqueror, on patrol south of the Falkland Islands, detected an Argentine oiler auxiliary which was accompanying the *Belgrano* on 30 April. She sighted the *Belgrano* for the first time on 1 May when it was accompanied by two destroyers armed with Exocet missiles. Paragraph 110 of Command 8758 describes the events of 2 May which led to the sinking of the cruiser. As Janet Young explained in the House of Lords on 13 July 1983, that account was not intended to say when the cruiser was first located. The essential point is that it was on 2 May that we had indications about the movements of the Argentine fleet which led the Task Force Commander, Admiral Woodward, to request a change in the Rules of Engagement to permit the *Belgrano* to be attacked outside the Total Exclusion Zone.

The circumstances on that day have been well described by Admiral Woodward in his lecture at the Royal United Services Institute on 20 October 1982:

> Early on the morning on 2 May, all the indications were that *25 De Mayo*, the Argentinian carrier, and a group of escorts had slipped past my forward SSN barrier to the north, while the cruiser *General Belgrano* and her escorts were attempting to complete the pincer movement from the south still outside the Total Exclusion Zone. But *Belgrano* still had *Conqueror* on the trail. My fear was that *Belgrano* would lose the SSN as she ran over the shallow water of the Burdwood Bank, and that my forward SSN barrier would be evaded down there too. I therefore sought, for the first and only time throughout the campaign, a major change to the

Rules of Engagement to enable *Conqueror* to attack
Belgrano outside the Exclusion Zone.

Ministers agreed to the proposed change in the Rules
of Engagement at about 1 pm London time on 2 May.
Orders were sent immediately to *HMS Conqueror*, which
attacked the *Belgrano* at 8 pm London time. Because of
the indications that the *Belgrano* posed a threat to the
Task Force, her precise position and course at the time
she was sunk were irrelevant.

The first indications of the possible Peruvian peace
proposals reached London from Washington at 11.15
pm London time and from Lima at 2 am London time
on 3 May.

My comments on paragraph 3 about the first contacts
with the *Belgrano* group go further than we have been
prepared to do hitherto. I have only felt able to do this
now as, with the passage of time, those events have lost
some of their original operational significance.

Throughout the events described above it was a major
concern of the Government to protect by all the means
available the Task Force which had been despatched to
the South Atlantic with all-party support.

Yours sincerely
Margaret Thatcher

The Right Hon. Denzil Davies, MP

For the first time this letter shifted the position of the
Government and by implication, though not directly,
admitted that earlier statements had been incorrect. But it too
contained a misleading statement. The letter implies that the
decision by the War Cabinet at Chequers on 2 May was
limited to allowing an attack on the *General Belgrano*. In
addition to try and justify a shift in position No. 10 had
introduced at the last moment a new paragraph into the letter
saying that the new information about the detection of the
cruiser had only been released now 'as, with the passage of
time, those events have lost some of their operational
significance'. This was not true. It had been known in MOD

for a year that the original information given on the time of
detection of the *General Belgrano* was wrong and that the
correct information was unclassified and could have been
made public.

The reply to Tam Dalyell

Now that the reply to Denzil Davies had been sent I turned to
dealing with the questions posed by Tam Dalyell. They all
involved fairly straightforward factual information. Now that
the correct information had been given about the time of first
detection and sighting of the cruiser there were no problems
about giving out information on its position and course up
until the time it was attacked. But to double check I sent my
draft reply to members of the naval and intelligence staffs and
they confirmed that the information was not classified. On 12
April I sent the proposed reply to Michael Heseltine via John
Stanley. I pointed out that the information was not classified
and although part of the reply would reveal for the first time
that the *General Belgrano* had reversed course away from the
Task Force at 9 am on 2 May the complete reply would not be
unhelpful to the Government. I did not supply a vast range of
arguments in favour of answering the letter because at the
meetings with Michael Heseltine over the weekend of 30
March–1 April it had been agreed that a new policy of more
openness was being adopted. After setting out the background of the Prime Minister's reply to Denzil Davies on 4
April I suggested that the four crucial questions from Tam
Dalyell should be answered as follows:

Question:
   At what time on 30 April 1982 did *HMS Conqueror* first
   detect the *Belgrano* on its sonar? What was the estimated
   position, course and speed of the *Belgrano* at the time?
Answer:
   As the Prime Minister has pointed out, *HMS Conqueror*
   did not detect the *General Belgrano* on its sonar on 30
   April 1982; it made contact with an accompanying oiler
   auxiliary.

Question:

At what time did *HMS Conqueror* come into visual contact with the *Belgrano* on 1 May 1982 and what was the course, speed and position of the *Belgrano* at the time?

Question:

At what time on 1 May 1982 did *HMS Conqueror* observe the RAS (refuelling at sea) involving the *Belgrano* and oiler and what was the course, speed and position of the *Belgrano* at the time?

Answer:

Again as the Prime Minister has already said, the first visual contact with *Belgrano* was at 2 pm London time on 1 May. At the time *Belgrano* was conducting a RAS with the oiler. The position at 3 pm London time was 54.07S 064.24W – Course 125, Speed 8 knots.

Question:

What was the course followed by the *Belgrano* throughout the period in which it was being tracked by *HMS Conqueror*?

Answer:

There is no continuous log of the *Belgrano*'s movements, but its position is known at certain times:

London time (2 May)	Position		Course	Speed (knots)
5 am	55.20S	060.14W	090	13
9 am	55.20S	057.22W	reversed course	
3 pm	55.16S	060.18W	270	14
8 pm	55.27S	061.25W	280	11

Some days later I saw the reply actually sent to Tam Dalyell by Michael Heseltine on 18 April.

Thank you for your letter of 19 March asking some questions about the circumstances surrounding the sinking of the *General Belgrano*. Since you wrote this

letter, you have seen the Prime Minister's letter to
Denzil Davies of 4 April and you have yourself had a
further round of correspondence in your letter of 5 April
and the Prime Minister's reply of 12 April. There is
nothing that I can usefully add.

I was astounded by this abrupt reversal of the decision
taken only a couple of weeks earlier to at last start telling the
truth. The cover up was obviously in full swing again. *I had
never come across anything so blatant in my fifteen years in the
Civil Service. It was a deliberate attempt to conceal information
which would reveal that Ministers had gravely misled
Parliament for the previous two years.* Knowledge of what
Ministers had decided was widespread and not confined to
those who had attended the previous meetings. It included
other departments such as the Foreign Office yet not a single
senior civil servant above me made the slightest comment or
protest about the sudden change of policy and the response to
Tam Dalyell. The reply sent was highly misleading. The
Prime Minister's letter to Denzil Davies of 4 April did not
actually deal with any of the points raised by Tam Dalyell,
and it was disingenuous of Heseltine to say that 'there is
nothing that I can usefully add'. But at least he had not tried
to claim security as a ground for refusing to provide the
information. That was to come later.

In the Civil Service a letter like this from a Minister would
be – and indeed was – taken as a statement of policy on how to
handle questions on the sinking. Michael Heseltine made it
clear in the evidence he gave to the Foreign Affairs
Committee on 7 November 1984 why he took the decision to
continue the cover up:

It was apparent to me that if we were to move down the
route of following the detailed analysis which was being
requested of the Ministry in questions to me, we would
end up with yet more requests for yet more information ... it was quite apparent to me that the more
information that we provided the more it would fuel yet
more demands for more information.

As a civil servant I was used to seeing drafts rejected or heavily modified. That is just a fact of life in a bureaucracy. But this was something different. Ministers had decided to continue to mislead Parliament. The cover up now looked as though it was bound to continue. Consistency not truth was to be the order of the day. I found myself wondering whether the Civil Service was really going to be party to the deliberate deception of Parliament simply to try and preserve the illusion that Ministers had told the truth and thus protect their political reputation.

I took my first decision – and it was a rather lonely one. I could not, to be frank, bring myself to disclose Government information. It went against all my training. I therefore appeased my conscience by sending Dalyell on 24 April an unsigned note. In it, I told him that the answers to his questions were unclassified and that he should press them. Dalyell tabled questions 2, 3 and 4 in his letter of 19 March as Parliamentary Questions together with a general one to the Prime Minister about the sequence of events on 30 April–2 May 1982. The general rules for answering such questions are that if the information is unclassified and easily available then there is no option but to provide it. Accordingly I submitted draft replies to John Stanley that followed the same line as in the letter Heseltine had refused to send to Tam Dalyell. These replies were sent to John Stanley on 2 May. Later that day Dalyell was suspended from the Commons for five days for using 'unparliamentary language' – he had called the Prime Minister a liar. His Parliamentary questions were likely to lapse as a result of the suspension but other events were in train that were to bring the arguments inside MOD to a head.

On 1 May Tam Dalyell had written a further letter to Michael Heseltine. He had seen through Heseltine's evasive reply and he still wanted the facts. The text of his letter was:

Dear Michael,
Thank you for your letter of 18 April concerning my questions on the circumstances surrounding the sinking of the *General Belgrano*.

While I appreciate the comments concerning the correspondence with the Prime Minister, my questions to you were of a specific nature which concern your Ministry.

I would therefore appreciate a reply to those questions from you.

Yours sincerely

Tam Dalyell

The letter was sent down for me to draft a response. Clearly Heseltine's private office expected me to provide a reply similar to the one that had been sent on 18 April. I decided to think carefully about whether I was prepared to offer my 'advice' in this form.

In a busy operations Defence Secretariat like DS5 there is hardly time to sit and think deeply about what you are doing and why. Much of the time it's probably unnecessary anyway. And there isn't a detailed 'rule book' to tell you what to do. But I did remember that the first major lesson I had learnt on joining the Civil Service fifteen years before had been 'you must never lie to Parliament'. This meant two things, my boss had told me – you certainly must not tell a deliberate lie, and if inadvertently the Minister gets the facts wrong then he must put the record straight immediately. The MOD instructions on answering Parliamentary questions simply say that even the smallest mistake in an answer can gravely damage the reputation of the Minister and the department.

Whilst I was still contemplating what I should do I received a minute by John Stanley's Private Secretary. Nobody else in the Ministry received a copy. From the minute it was clear that Ministers had been discussing how to deal with Tam Dalyell. The sequence of events that was painted in the document is an interesting portrait of Whitehall at work. For, on receiving my draft answers to Dalyell's questions, John Stanley had gone round to talk to

Michael Heseltine. The latter had suggested that all Dalyell's questions should be answered by saying:

> I have nothing to add to the letter to the Rt Hon Member for Llanelli (Denzil Davies) from my Rt Hon Friend the Prime Minister and my subsequent letter to the Hon Member (Dalyell) of 18 April.

This was a repetition of the previous line taken by Heseltine – a refusal to answer but with no reason given. John Stanley was clearly dissatisfied with this sort of reply. He still hankered after blocking all questions by using national security as an excuse. He decided to discuss the issue with No. 10. As a result, the reply he wanted to use was:

> It is not our practice to comment on military operational matters (or details of military operations). The circumstances leading to the sinking of the *Belgrano* were described in my letter to the Rt Hon Member for Llanelli (Denzil Davies) of 4 April.

This line was also to be the basis on which 'subsequent Questions on the *Belgrano*'s movements on 1 and 2 May can be answered'.

This intervention by John Stanley was now a move from a failure to provide information to a deliberate attempt to mislead. The reply he suggested was false in two respects. First, it is perfectly normal practice to comment on many aspects of military operational matters. Indeed the Prime Minister had just provided details about the *General Belgrano* to Denzil Davies. Second, the information about the sinking was not classified, dealing as it did with events exactly two years earlier. What Stanley wanted was to use national security as an excuse for not releasing to Parliament information which was simply politically embarrassing. Yet the military advice was that the information Dalyell wanted was not classified.

The Arguments for the Truth

The whole argument about misleading Parliament had to be faced. Heseltine wanted a letter that would tell Dalyell that no further information would be forthcoming. Stanley wanted my agreement to his proposed use of national security as a blanket to cover up the fact that members of the Government had misled the House of Commons for two years. I finally decided that I could not be a party to this sort of behaviour by Ministers. I sat down at my desk on 9 May 1984 and wrote out the strongest minute I ever sent in my Civil Service career. To those unaccustomed to Civil Service drafting it may appear to be formal in tone and restrained in language, but that is how Whitehall works. This minute was nonetheless designed to be a clear signal to everybody above me in the chain that I was not prepared to carry out the Ministerial instructions I had just received. The first paragraph of the minute set out the background for those who would not be familiar with all that had taken place. The second paragraph made it clear what I thought of the policy Ministers wanted to adopt:

Minister (AF) (John Stanley) has suggested, following a discussion with No. 10, that all the questions, in particular the PQs, should be answered as follows:

'It is not our practice to comment on military operational matters [or the details of military operations]. The circumstances leading to the sinking of the *Belgrano* were described in my (the PM's) letter to the Rt Hon Member for Llanelli (Denzil Davies) of 4 April'.

Unfortunately I do not believe that it is possible to sustain this line. We have already given substantial information about the *Belgrano*, including its position and course when attacked, and the Prime Minister has recently confirmed the date of the first detection of the group and the first sighting of the *Belgrano*. The information on the position of the *Belgrano* when first sighted and its course up until the time it was attacked is unclassified and available without disproportionate effort and in accordance with the normal rules for answering PQs there is no reason for withholding this information. I can therefore only advise that we should stick to the original answers to the PQs which I submitted on 2 May.

I concluded by saying:

There are also sound tactical reasons for answering the questions posed by Mr Dalyell in his letter rather than allowing the information to emerge in pieces via PQs. The four PQs tabled by Mr Dalyell will reveal that *Belgrano* reversed course at 9 am London time but the advantage of answering his letter is that the answer to question 7 enables us to bring out the very limited contacts with *HMS Conqueror*. Without this answer the reply to question 4 on the course of the *Belgrano* could give a misleading impression of the information available in London when the ROEs were changed. A draft to Tam Dalyell is attached and as I suggested in my earlier minute you may wish to clear this with No. 10 and a draft is attached.

Stanley disagreed and told Heseltine that he would have 'no difficulty' in claiming the information was classified, even though it wasn't and that the reply showed 'the depth of water the Secretary of State would be in if he were to send it'. The 'depth of water' referred to the exposure of the 'cover up' and the way Ministers had misled Parliament.

None of my superiors intervened; I received no support from anybody else in the Ministry. Obviously they were content to do what Ministers wanted even if this meant being party to a 'cover up'. Heseltine accepted that the information Dalyell wanted was unclassified but refused to send it anyway. Later I saw the reply that Heseltine actually sent to Tam Dalyell on 14 May.

Thank you for your further letter of 1 May.

Your purpose in asking the questions you put to me is to pursue your campaign that the *Belgrano* was attacked in order to destroy the prospects for peace negotiations rather than for the military reason that she posed a threat to the Task Force. I do not believe that there is any point in prolonging this argument by a further round of detailed correspondence.

There had, of course, been no 'argument' – the new evasive Heseltine ploy was to throw in accusations about the Peruvian peace plan to cover up his unwillingness to reveal how Parliament had been misled. A fortnight later the indefatigable Dalyell wrote another long letter to Michael Heseltine asking more detailed questions. This time Heseltine's office did not even bother to ask me to provide a reply. No doubt by now they knew what I would say.

The letter from Dalyell is very interesting. He rightly asks where any of the information he has asked for is in the earlier replies from either the Prime Minister and Heseltine. He then puts his finger on the two main issues, both of which were to be central to my Old Bailey trial. First Dalyell says, absolutely correctly: 'It's not that you can't easily answer the questions: it is rather that you don't want to.' Second, the fundamental constitutional issue: 'Does this not raise important issues about being Ministerially accountable to Parliament?' The full text of the important part of this letter is:

Where in Denzil Davies' letter from the Prime Minister of 4 April, or for that matter anywhere else in the House or in Ministry of Defence Statements are the answers to my questions of 19 March to be found? You know perfectly well that it is not a question of getting your civil servants to do voluminous research – it is a simple matter of reference to the log-book of the *Conqueror*. It's not that you can't easily answer the questions: it is rather that you don't want to.

But there is a wider issue. Irrespective of new facts that emerge about the sinking of the *Belgrano*, and new information coming from members of the Task Force and others, are we to take it that Defence Ministers will be refusing to reply?

Does this not raise important issues about being Ministerially accountable to Parliament? Was it on the advice of your officials that the questions I posed in my letter have not been answered? I would be surprised if it were so, since I have a high regard for the industry and integrity of Ministry of Defence officials with whom I have dealt, and have found that they regard answering serious questions from MPs, who themselves have worked on a topic, as part of their day-to-day job.

On 11 June Michael Heseltine sent another rude reply to Tam Dalyell:

Thank you for your letter of 27 May about your questions on the sinking of the *Belgrano*.

You refer to the Diary piece in the *Sunday Times* which claimed that I was not prepared to answer your questions because to do so would waste the time of my officials. In fact I have never suggested that it would be disproportionately expensive to deal with the questions you have posed in our recent correspondence: cost is not the consideration.

Rather, my refusal to answer the many detailed questions you have put to me, to which you have now added some more in your latest letter, rests on the fact that, as I said in my letter of 14 May to you, your purpose is to pursue your campaign to demonstrate your belief that the *Belgrano* was attacked in order to destroy the prospects for peace negotiations and not because she posed a threat to the Task Force. Since, as the Prime Minister made clear yet again in her letter of 12 April to you, your contention is simply not true, I remain of the view that there is nothing to be gained from providing the detailed answers you are seeking.

At least he did not try to claim the information was classified or not available but simply that there would be 'nothing to be gained from providing the detailed answers you are seeking'. Neither did he use the argument advanced endlessly by the Government later that national security was at stake. Obviously Michael Heseltine did not have anything to gain by providing truthful answers but Parliament certainly had something to gain by being told how it had been misled. Events were now moving inside Parliament that were finally to bring the issue to a head and present me with the most difficult decision I ever had to take.

The Deception of the Foreign Affairs Committee

The House of Commons Foreign Affairs Committee had started an enquiry into the future of the Falkland Islands and the prospect for a negotiated solution to the problem. As part of this enquiry the Committee considered some of the unsuccessful attempts to secure a settlement during the conflict. This led them to look into the Peruvian peace plan and this inevitably involved the question of the possible linkage with the sinking of the *General Belgrano*. On 11 June 1984 the former Foreign Secretary, Francis Pym, gave evidence to the Committee. In the course of questioning by the Labour MP Nigel Spearing on the sequence of events on 2 May 1982 and the decision by the War Cabinet to change the rules of engagement Francis Pym said:

> It was one of many changes made in the course of the war and one that in my absence I would certainly support the War Cabinet in making.

The following week, on 20 June, Baroness Young, Minister of State in the Foreign Office, appeared before the Committee and was asked about the evidence given by Francis Pym. Nigel Spearing asked her to provide 'a note of the other changes which took place and the dates and the outcome of these changes'. Baroness Young agreed to let the Committee have such a note. The request for this information was then made formally by the Clerk to the Committee in a letter to the Foreign Office on 28 June. Amongst other items it specifically asked for a list of 'all changes in the Rules of Engagement issued to HM Forces in the South Atlantic between 2 April and 15 June 1982 and confirming the accuracy of Mr Pym's statement to the

Committee on 11 June that changes in the Rules of Engagement "happened quite a number of times in the course of the war".' This request could only be answered by MOD and so it was transferred by the Foreign Office to my colleague, Michael Legge, the Head of the division responsible for general policy on operations outside the NATO area.

The 'Legge Minute'

Defence Ministers had already made it very clear how requests for this sort of information should be handled and Michael Legge accordingly prepared a paper to go to the Select Committee in line with the stated Ministerial policy. This he sent to John Stanley's office on Friday, 6 July. I saw my copy of this minute in the middle of Monday morning, 9 July. I was very concerned at what I read. The crucial paragraphs are:

HOUSE OF COMMONS FOREIGN AFFAIRS COMMITTEE: SOUTH ATLANTIC ROE

We have discussed the form of our response with the Defence Commitments Staff, DS5 and DNW who had particular responsibility for ROE during Operation Corporate. We have also borne in mind the statements made to date by Ministers on the subject of the *Belgrano*. Our advice is that we should *not* provide the Committee with a note listing all the changes. There are a number of reasons for this. Firstly the ROE themselves are classified, and are drawn from the Fleet Operating and Tactical Instructions which is a classified document. The Committee have indicated that they would prefer the note to be unclassified. Secondly some of the ROE are still in force for our Falklands garrison. Thirdly the production of a full list of all changes would be an extremely time-consuming exercise, not only because of the difficulty of assembling the information from departmental records, but also because the ROE would have to be paraphrased at some length since their format would be almost incomprehensible to the layman. In addition a full list of changes would provide more information than Ministers have been prepared to reveal so far about the *Belgrano* affair. For instance, the list of changes in the period 20 April–7 May would show that the engagement of the Argentine aircraft carrier *25 De Mayo* outside the Total Exclusion Zone was permitted from 30 April, and that the change on 2 May was not restricted to *Belgrano* but included all Argentine warships over a large area. It would also reveal that whilst the public warnings and ROE changes for the MEZ and TEZ were simultaneous, there was a delay until 7 May before the appropriate warning was issued for the 2 May change.

I therefore recommend that we should avoid these difficulties by providing the Committee with a more general narrative, explaining broadly when changes were made to ROE, but emphasising that changes were a continual and routine process, thus confirming the thrust of Mr Pym's evidence. I attach a draft on these lines. Since it does not actually specify any ROE it would pose no problems from a security point of view. It is consistent with previous official statements by Ministers and others, including Admiral Woodward, about the change of ROE which led to the sinking of the *Belgrano*. The draft deliberately avoids any reference to the underlying system of ROE or the mechanism for their approval, since neither aspect was touched by Mr Spearing.

My eye was caught by the statement that the note requested by the Committee was not going to be provided. This was unusual since normally requests from a Parliamentary committee are answered as fully as possible. I read carefully through the reasons given by Michael Legge. The first and second reasons that the rules of engagement are classified is not strictly correct since if they were paraphrased to make them intelligible any classified material would be removed. Even if some classified material remained this did not preclude it being shown to a Select Committee since they often see classified material. The third reason that providing the list would be a time-consuming exercise whilst correct is hardly a compelling reason for not answering the questions posed by the Committee and indeed Michael Heseltine did, before the end of 1984, provide all the information the Committee wanted. The real reason for withholding the details that the Select Committee wanted came last:

> A full list of the changes would provide more information than Ministers have been prepared to reveal so far about the *Belgrano* affair.

This advice was fully in line with the directions given by Michael Heseltine and John Stanley in April and May about the way information should be released to Parliament. But this was going a stage further than the refusal to provide information to a persistent backbench MP. *Ministers were now involved in blocking an enquiry by a Select Committee which had the right to enquire and get truthful answers. Ministers were also going to provide a misleading memorandum that would at best be 'consistent with previous statements' and which had the clear purpose of blocking any further enquiries.*

The Moment of Truth

I considered carefully what I should do. My first thought was to write a note of dissent to John Stanley but recalling how my arguments and advice had already been rejected or ignored twice it was obvious that Ministers were not suddenly going to change their minds (or values) now and adopt a more forthcoming position. I had received no support for 'coming clean' and putting the record straight before from those higher up in the department including Sir Clive Whitmore and I did not expect any now. I wondered about appealing to somebody outside the department, but I remembered that the Prime Minister had been consulted over the earlier decisions and there was nobody independent to whom I could appeal. It was clear that all the methods of effective protest inside the department or the Civil Service

were cut off by people already involved in the 'cover up'.
Ministers were determined to stop *any* more information
about the events surrounding the sinking of the *General
Belgrano* becoming public. My last hope was that Ministers
would realise what they were doing, *think* about their
responsibility to Parliament and change their minds at the
last moment. I put the minute from Michael Legge on one
side and waited to see what would happen.

I did not have to wait very long. John Stanley wrote to
Michael Heseltine saying that he, Stanley, agreed with the
proposals and asking for Heseltine's agreement to send the
memorandum to the Select Committee. About a day later
Heseltine agreed. Stanley then signed the memorandum and
sent it off to the Select Committee on the 13 July 1984.

I then realised that I was going to have to act and somehow
tell Parliament the true situation. I took a copy of the minute
from Michael Legge to John Stanley and kept it at work.
When I went home that Friday evening I knew I had to
decide that weekend what to do. My mind went back over the
events that had taken place since I arrived as Head of DS5 in
March: the writing of the 'Crown Jewels', the discovery of
the cover up, the meetings with Heseltine and Stanley, the
refusal to tell Dalyell the truth which would reveal how
extensively Parliament had been misled, and now the
involvement of the Foreign Affairs Committee. It dawned on
me that I was about the only person who knew all that had
happened. Whether I liked it or not I would have to decide
what to do. Could I really bring myself to send the documents
to Parliament? All my instincts after fifteen years in the Civil
Service told me that my loyalty was to Ministers and the
department. But then I realised that Ministers had broken
their side of the bargain in attempting to evade their
responsibilities to Parliament. If they could just simply shrug
off their duties, refuse to answer questions, give misleading
answers or refuse to correct false statements to Parliament
how could there be any effective control over what the
Government did? In the end Ministers had to be responsible
to Parliament or the whole British constitutional system

would break down. It never occurred to me to send the papers to the newspapers. This was a matter for Parliament.

If I sent the papers to Parliament where should I send them? If I was to reveal how Parliament had been deceived then clearly the letter I had twice tried to persuade Heseltine to send to Dalyell was highly relevant because it showed that numerous earlier statements by the Government were not true. One possibility was that I could send the papers to Sir Anthony Kershaw, the chairman of the Foreign Affairs Committee. As I thought about this I realised that the Committee had only just started to investigate the sinking of the *General Belgrano* and even then only as part of another enquiry. They did not know all the background and might not understand the significance of the information. So I decided that Tam Dalyell would be the right person. He had been consistently misled almost every time he asked a question about the sinking and he knew more than anybody else outside MOD about the events. I was sure he would understand the significance of the information and realise the importance of passing on to the Foreign Affairs Committee what they needed to know.

I spent most of the weekend turning over in my mind the question of what I should do. By the Sunday evening I had decided that Parliament had to be told what was happening and what had taken place over the previous two years. If I sent the papers I knew that I would be breaking the written and unwritten rules of the Civil Service but that no longer seemed to be important. But would I be breaking the Official Secrets Act? My mind went back to my previous job and my efforts to try and understand the long and complicated wording of Section 2 of the Act with its obscure reference to 'duty in the interests of the State'. I could not see how telling Parliament that it had been and was being misled could be contrary to the 'interests of the State'.

Then I suddenly remembered this had cropped up in a book that had been given to me by Sir Derek Rayner when I had worked for him on the efficiency drive in Whitehall five years before. The book was *Your Disobedient Servant* by

Leslie Chapman and was about his attempts to improve efficiency in the Property Services Agency. He had been unsuccessful but after he had left the Civil Service and published the first edition of the book it was revealed that information given by his Permanent Secretary, Sir Robert Cox, to the Public Accounts Committee, had been false. The Public Accounts Committee had called Sir Robert Cox back to give further evidence and explain how and why he had misled the Committee. During the questioning one MP raised the possibility that any civil servant who revealed that his superiors had given misleading information to Parliament might be prosecuted under the Official Secrets Act. The Government eventually provided a note to explain the position and reassure Parliament that the truth would not be concealed. That note is printed in the Penguin edition of Leslie Chapman's book, which was still on a shelf in my study. It reads:

OFFICIAL SECRETS ACT

Note by the Treasury

The Committee have asked whether it would be a breach of the Official Secrets Act for an official who believes that misleading evidence has been given to the Committee by one of his senior officers to publicise his opinion of the facts . . .

If the officer without authorisation published the facts (as distinct from his opinion of facts already public), such publication could, depending upon the precise circumstances, amount to a breach of Section 2 of the 1911 Act. *There would, of course, be no such breach if the sole publication were to the Committee or to the House since the publication would in that event amount to a proceeding in Parliament and would be absolutely privileged.*

Prosecutions under the Official Secrets Act require the Attorney-General's consent . . . No prosecution has been brought under the 1911 Act in the circumstances that the Committee have in mind.

When I read this I realised that this referred to exactly the circumstances I found myself in. Indeed I was faced not with officials misleading Parliament but Ministers themselves. I had already tried to get senior officials in MOD to take action. They had opted out. It was now up to me. I had only ever intended to send the information to Parliament and here was confirmation that I would not be breaching the Official Secrets Act. It was clear what I had to do.

When I arrived at work on the Monday morning I took a copy of the letter that should have gone to Tam Dalyell. I put this together with the copy of the minute to John Stanley into the envelope I had already typed. That lunchtime I posted them to Tam Dalyell. I had no regrets about what I had done. But events were now outside my hands. What would Parliament do when they found out the truth about what Ministers had told them?

CHAPTER SIX

PROSECUTION

I sent the documents to Tam Dalyell on 16 July 1984. Within ten days they were back inside the Ministry of Defence. How had this happened? I found out much later that when Tam Dalyell received the documents he thought long and hard about what he should do. He had clear evidence that he had been deceived; even more important that the Foreign Affairs Committee had been deceived. He decided that the papers should be placed before the Committee so that they could see how they had been misled by MOD. When the Committee saw the papers they agreed that Michael Heseltine should be asked to give evidence to explain what was happening. They also agreed to hand back to Heseltine the papers they had received from Tam Dalyell. This was an extraordinary decision by a Select Committee of the House of Commons which had been misled by the Government. Where was Parliament's old ability and duty to stand up to the Executive and assert its rights? Tam Dalyell says he was 'aghast' at the Committee's action.

The chairman of the Foreign Affairs Committee, Sir Anthony Kershaw, went to see Heseltine on 26 July. In return for giving back the papers he extracted a promise that Heseltine would come down to Parliament and give evidence to the Committee. Once Kershaw had departed, Heseltine called in the MOD police. Within days they had started an enquiry to try and trace the 'leak'.

The MOD police are a peculiar body, nominally independent under their own Chief Constable but actually closely controlled by the department. Two officers were in charge of the enquiry, Chief Inspector Hughes and Inspector

Broome. They had some forensic work done on the documents and arrived to start investigations in my division, DS5, in the afternoon of Wednesday, 8 August. They took some samples from the photocopier in the division and disappeared. After all the protests I had made it probably didn't take them long to identify the chief suspect. In the middle of the Friday afternoon, 10 August, they asked me to go up and see them in the office they had taken over on the sixth floor of the MOD building. This was the start of a series of events that many of those involved had great difficulty in recalling precisely when they later made statements and appeared as witnesses. These events became, after my acquittal, the subject of acute political controversy about the role Ministers played in the decision to prosecute me. At the trial I said that an understanding had been reached that my resignation would be the end of the matter. Prosecution witnesses denied this, although they agreed I had written a letter of resignation late that afternoon. They also claimed that I had tried to blame my colleagues for the leak. I denied this strongly at the Old Bailey.

As I left the building I was asked to come back on the Tuesday to sign off the various access forms to highly classified information and sort out the administrative details. I left the MOD knowing that my own career in the Civil Service was over but also believing that I had a clear agreement that the whole affair was closed. I still had no regrets about what I had done and no complaints about the outcome. As I came through the door I remember telling my wife Sally that I was now 'unemployed'.

What happened next was revealed in September in an extraordinary 'leak' to the Labour leader, Neil Kinnock, from someone very highly placed inside MOD who was clearly upset and angry about what had taken place. On Monday, 13 August, Sir Ewan Broadbent first spoke to the DPP and then travelled down to Michael Heseltine's country house in Oxfordshire. He reported that the 'leak' investigation was over and that I had confessed to sending the documents. He also told Heseltine that the Chief Constable of the MOD police did not recommend prosecution. National security was not involved and the papers had only gone to Parliament and in addition they were embarrassing for the department. Heseltine said he personally favoured a prosecution, but would leave a final decision to the Attorney-General. If there was no prosecution he wanted me dismissed. Mrs Thatcher was informed later that day.

The next day (14 August) I went in to MOD to see Hastie-Smith, the Head of Personnel at MOD. As I said in evidence, I recollect him saying – although he was later to dispute my recollection:

> I'm very sorry, Clive, this is not going as smoothly as we hoped. Ministers are jumping up and down. They've insisted that we put the papers to the DPP. However, we're still convinced this is not a matter for the Official Secrets Act and that we shall be able to accept your resignation by the end of the week. But it might come to an internal disciplinary hearing and I think you ought to go to the FDA and get some help.

I was then told that my resignation, though accepted on Friday, no longer applied and I was being suspended without pay. The next few days were agonising waiting to find out what would happen, though I expected the worst. I went to see John Ward, the General Secretary of my union, the FDA (First Division Association), who then lobbied inside Whitehall against a prosecution. But it was too late. The papers reached Sir Thomas Hetherington, the Director of Public Prosecutions, late on Thursday, 16 August. He spoke to Hughes and Broome about their report. The next day the DPP spoke to the Solicitor-General, Sir Patrick Mayhew. There was then a brief discussion over the telephone with the Attorney-General, Sir Michael Havers, who was on holiday in France. They had few papers in front of them. Havers decided on a prosecution.

An hour after this brief exchange Inspector Broome

arrived at my house in Islington to arrest me. I was taken off to Canon Row Police Station, duly fingerprinted and photographed and finally charged. At the end of the whole process a team of officers from the Special Branch arrived outside, alerted no doubt by a charge under the Official Secrets Act and anxious to talk to me about my political beliefs. They knew nothing about the facts of the case. Inspector Broome stoutly refused to let them talk to me and after a lot of argument I was released.

At 10 o'clock that evening the front doorbell rang. Sally opened the door to find a *Daily Mail* journalist anxious to know how she felt about the fact that her husband was 'in a spot of trouble with the police'. Then our telephone rang. It was the *Daily Star* asking similar questions. Within minutes the street was swarming with reporters and photographers. We said nothing. How had the story got out and so quickly? An article next day in the *Daily Mail* said that 'Special Branch officers were treating their enquiries as a matter of the utmost seriousness'. We then had a frantic time telling our families what had happened before they heard on the TV or read the newspapers. It had been a bad day for the family. My sister-in-law had died of cancer that morning.

The following day, Saturday, 18 August, I appeared at Bow Street Magistrates Court in order to secure an extension of the unconditional bail. The court was packed. Unconditional bail was immediately granted and thirty seconds later it was all over. Inspector Broome kindly arranged for us to leave from the adjacent police station in a police van, met us in his car and took us home.

Within half an hour of returning home our house was under siege from the media. We escaped by climbing over the six foot garden wall to our neighbours at the back where my brother-in-law picked us up in his car. The rest of the weekend was a series of rapid family conferences and we took refuge with friends on Saturday night. After all that had happened I felt absolutely determined to defend myself against what I saw as a political prosecution. I was determined to fight back; exactly how would be decided over the next few days. Our only minor triumph that weekend was to evade the press photographers.

Meanwhile events were moving elsewhere. Tam Dalyell heard the news of my arrest early on the Saturday morning. Late in the evening the first editions of the *Observer* ran an exclusive story, 'BELGRANO COVER UP EXPOSED', with the details of how vital information on the sinking had been withheld from the Foreign Affairs Committee. Fleet Street had already put two and two together and the *Observer* ran the story of my appearance in court on the front page exactly opposite the *Belgrano* story. Even on the Monday morning the *Guardian* was still leading with the story and clearly it was now a major political issue with a momentum of its own.

My first concern was to get a lawyer and start fighting the case. It was at this stage that I received offers of help from Duncan Campbell of the *New Statesman* and David Leigh of the *Observer*. Duncan had himself been through a trial under the Official Secrets Act (as described in Chapter 1) and David was also well informed, having written a book on Official Secrecy. After talking to them about possible solicitors and consulting John Ward of the FDA and Marie Staunton and Barbara Cohen of NCCL, I decided to go to Bindman and Partners, a well-known firm of radical lawyers. Brian Raymond, their senior partner on criminal law, agreed to take the case. Over the next five months I was to work very closely with Brian and we rapidly became good friends. Throughout he showed tremendous dedication as he put in very long hours developing the defence. He also showed great flair in handling the huge and continuing interest shown in my case by the Press and media generally.

At our first meeting Brian and I decided that we could certainly use the 'interests of the State' defence. How we would do it we would consider in more detail later. Our first aim was to make public the real nature of the charges I faced. We decided to run an exclusive story with David Leigh in the *Observer* a week after my first appearance in court. The *Observer* wanted a photograph and a statement and so suddenly I had to get used to the attentions of the media and how to handle them.

Brian and I realised that the Government would want to present the whole case as a 'sordid little leak' and we recognised the need to try and win the public debate in advance of the trial which we guessed would not be before early 1985.

At the beginning of September I discovered that not only was my phone being tapped but that all my correspondence was being opened. Big Brother was watching me in 1984 after all. My bank statement arrived late and had so obviously been tampered with, leaving creases and glue all over the back of the envelope, that it may even have been intended as a warning. No doubt the Government were trying to find out if newspapers (or even more sinister agencies!) had been paying me money. I had nothing to hide but it is a disconcerting feeling that the Special Branch are reading every piece of mail first. So as well as being cautious about conversations – especially about our playing of the defence legal strategy – on the phone (and I shall never know if the tapping is stopped) we now had to be circumspect about the mail too. They must have wasted hours of tape and time listening in to all the sympathetic calls we had throughout those weeks from our family and friends.

On 12 September Brian and I had our first conference with my junior counsel, Jonathan Caplan, one of the most brilliant younger members of the Bar. For the first time we discussed in detail how we might construct an 'interests of the State' defence. We all realised that we were on new legal ground – this defence had never been used before in the history of the 1911 Act. There was clearly much work for Jonathan to do, researching possible legal precedents.

The next day I made my first real appearance in court. Bow Street was packed with cameras and photographers and we fought our way in surrounded by a dozen large policemen. That morning the *Guardian* Diary had carried an item recording a meeting of Whitehall information officers at which Mrs Thatcher's press secretary, Bernard Ingham, was reported to have said that the Government was 'quite set' upon prosecution. Indeed it was hoped that 'an appropriately severe member of the judiciary would be on hand to hear the case'. This looked like yet another piece of political interference – a process that had started in August and was to be repeated right up to the start of the trial. In a crowded courtroom at the end of a busy morning, Brian Raymond asked, to the great surprise of the representative from the DPP, for reporting restrictions to be lifted, handed up a copy of the article and said:

> If what is said is correct and the Prime Minister's personal press secretary has asked for this matter to be listed before a severe judge it constitutes a serious interference with the process of justice.

The next day all the newspapers carried the story. The *Daily Mail* headline was, 'DOWNING STREET INTERFERED IN CHOICE OF JUDGE' and even the *Sun* said, 'SECRET BID TO FIX LEAK CASE'.

On a personal level all our holiday plans for the summer had to be abandoned once I had been charged and we also had to adjust our planned spending (Hastie-Smith had written to tell me I was now being suspended on half pay). But Sally and I both needed a break and so we left London in late September for a week to stay in a friend's cottage near the North York Moors. The level of media attention was such that even this mundane fact was reported in the *Times* Diary.

Just before going on holiday I had met Des Wilson, the Chairman of the Freedom of Information Campaign, which had decided to back our fight against the prosecution and organise my defence fund to help pay the legal expenses. The National Council of Civil Liberties joined as a sponsor organisation. Perhaps more surprisingly the First Division Association also agreed to be a sponsor. This was a very courageous decision. Des Wilson also obtained the agreement of all three Opposition party leaders – Neil Kinnock, David Owen and David Steel – to act as patrons of the fund. This was an unprecedented move – never before had the party leaders been prepared to come out in favour of a civil servant who had been accused of 'leaking'. The thousands of contributions to the fund were a tangible sign that ordinary people did care about the issues in the case.

Meanwhile the press coverage continued to grow. The comment I enjoyed most of all came in a 'Dear Bill' letter from Denis Thatcher in *Private Eye*:

> Did you see that uppity quack Owen has been sounding off about the *Belgrano*. My advice was to come clean and say what the hell is war about if it's not torpedoeing a boatload of Argies before they steam in and do the same to us, but for the Boss this is a very sore point, her finest hour, etc, and any word of criticism brings on the heebie-jeebies. In this I think she was encouraged by Tarzan, and they have now decided to string up some little Whitehall paper-pusher, rack, thumbscrews, the whole works, just because he photostated a few memos and sent them down to Halitosis Hall.

We now had to turn our attention to the committal proceedings at Bow Street on 9 October. We had no realistic expectation of getting the prosecution case thrown out. We concentrated instead on establishing some important points for the trial. The main weapon of the prosecution would obviously be the disputed records of my conversations with the MOD police on 10 August. We decided that if that was the worse they could do we might as well let it come out at the committal since it would then seem stale at the real trial. Our main objective was to start constructing a public interest defence.

Roy Amlot opened the proceedings for the prosecution in a low-key way. He made the most of the contested account of my interview with the police, but he made a very important statement that the two documents sent to Tam Dalyell were a breach of confidence though there was 'no suggestion of any damage to national security'. Hastie-Smith then gave evidence. Under cross-examination by Jonathan Caplan he gradually admitted some of the events of 10 August. He agreed that I had resigned and much to the amazement of Roy Amlot the MOD police produced my resignation letter. Hastie-Smith's memory was very good about the sequence of events, but did not coincide with mine about what had been said. He denied that there had been a deal.

Richard Mottram gave evidence and with no reluctance confirmed all the details about internal MOD meetings and minutes that we wanted to establish. This whole session probably seemed very strange to those present but it was a vital part of our longer term strategy. Jonathan Caplan made it clear that we did not accept the accuracy of the police record and I was committed for trial at the Old Bailey. As we left the court, pausing for the crowd of photographers, Brian Raymond read out a prepared statement:

> This afternoon's proceedings have made clear the nature of the prosecution case against Clive Ponting, the evidence which is to be called against him and the way in which that evidence is to be used. Mr Ponting's determination to contest these charges fully is, if anything, strengthened by today's events. I can confirm that he will be pleading not guilty.

After the committal proceedings I had to press on with a major research project for my legal team that I had started in September. This involved reading every *Hansard* from May 1982 until July 1984 and photocopying every reference to the *Belgrano* and the associated events, so putting together the full record of every misleading and untrue statement made to Parliament. In addition I was covering major newspaper articles, books and other background material. I was also writing a detailed history of the events in 1982 so that we had a comprehensive account on which to base that part of our case. This all took up an enormous amount of time and effort, mainly in the excellent Camden Reference Library on Euston Road. Suggestions on other possible avenues of research in legal, constitutional and other documents came to me or my lawyers from a variety of well-informed and helpful sources. Early in November 1984 Michael Heseltine was to give public evidence to the Foreign Affairs Committee about the *Belgrano*. On that morning the *Daily Mirror*, under the inches thick headline 'BELGRANO SENSATION', broke the story that the log-book of *HMS Conqueror* was missing. It seemed to illustrate vividly that there was indeed a 'cover up' underway. If classified Royal Navy documents were mysteriously disappearing more people would start to worry that something very peculiar was going on.

Brian Raymond and I decided to attend the Foreign Affairs Committee session to hear what Heseltine had to say. Although this meant more publicity it was not our real aim. These Parliamentary proceedings were vitally important for our defence. Members of the Committee asked Heseltine a series of detailed questions about the two documents I had sent to Tam Dalyell and, just as important, Heseltine answered the questions. The Committee made it clear that had they not had this information they would not have realised they had been misled by the Memorandum from MOD and they would not have pursued their enquiries.

In the middle of all these rows the Attorney-General, Sir Michael Havers, decided to intervene in my case again. Interviewed on the radio he first of all confirmed that the Government had doubts about the prosecution. We were also getting similar indications from other sources. Asked what was the public interest in continuing with the prosecution Havers said:

Well, I'm not sure. If you read all the comment and criticism that has happened since, it may be that the decision to prosecute is one that if considered by the Cabinet or by certain Cabinet Ministers they would have liked to have advised me another way.

Then in another extraordinary statement he added:

This is simply a question of a very senior civil servant disclosing matters which I say he had no right to disclose.

This commented on questions that still had to be decided

at the trial. As I happened to be driving along the M4 at the time with the radio on, such outspoken comments might well have stopped the case there and then as it was difficult to control the car and listen to such surprising remarks at the same time.

Brian and I decided that we should make a public response. Our letter rebuked the Attorney-General for making 'clear and categorical' statements about issues which still had to be proved and pointed out that:

> Unequivocal assertions of this nature coming from the senior law officer to whom the duty of restraining contempt is entrusted can only serve to increase public disquiet as to the fairness of the Government's conduct.

Havers responded that he had not committed contempt and that he had only described the basis on which the prosecution was brought. Brian replied that the letter was 'inconsistent with a proper regard for the rights of an accused person'. The intriguing question was since the Attorney-General was responsible for restraining contempt of court, would he prosecute himself for contempt? A difficult legal point no doubt. In the end Havers decided not to prosecute himself.

On 12 November at Commons Question Time the Attorney-General was asked by Michael Winnick whether he was aware of the considerable disquiet about my prosecution. Sir Michael Havers had to admit that:

> It would be impossible for anybody to be unaware of the considerable disquiet about my decision, since practically every newspaper and every radio and television broadcast on the subject has gone on and on about it.

But while all of this was going on and on we had to concentrate on developing the defence for the Old Bailey trial which had been set for the end of January under Mr Justice McCowan. We had spent a great deal of time discussing possible QCs, and the final decision had been made by Brian who felt it was most important to select the right advocate for a highly sensitive trial. When we announced our choice of Bruce Laughland he was described in the *Times* Diary as 'polite and elegant' and 'neither a tub thumper nor a member of the radical bar' and the choice was hailed as 'a clever piece of casting'. *The Times* also commented that this would be 'his most high-profile case and one of considerable constitutional importance'. I first met Bruce in the middle of November and immediately warmed to his dry sense of humour and the way in which he quickly grasped the complexities of the case from a few days' reading of a vast range of material.

We soon settled between us our strategic plan for fighting the case. A major problem was that we were inevitably dealing with a highly controversial issue on which the members of the jury were likely to have strong political views. It was no part of our case to refight the sinking of the *Belgrano* or whether the Peruvian peace plan had been deliberately torpedoed along with the *Belgrano*. We also had to fight within Section 2 as it was written. However widely discredited the Official Secrets Act was, it was still the law.

We thought that the jury might well feel, even after hearing all the evidence, that in some way I had broken the rules. We wanted an established political figure who had held high office to reassure the jury that my actions had been justified and bring home to them how vitally important it was for any Government to tell the truth to Parliament even if it was politically embarrassing. We spent a great deal of time searching for the right sort of person who would be prepared to appear as a witness in a highly publicised trial. We met with a variety of different reasons for refusing to appear, so I had better not mention any names. But we were eventually able to secure the witness we wanted – Merlyn Rees, who had been Home Secretary in the last Labour Government. This was a decision of great courage by Merlyn Rees since he had nothing to gain personally and had never been in the witness box at a criminal trial before. In the weeks before the trial he devoted a great deal of time in a series of conferences to working out the evidence he would give. In doing this we had invaluable and selfless help from Shirley Williams, the

President of the SDP, who came to all the conferences with Merlyn Rees. Our other key witness was to be a major expert on constitutional law, and that fortunately proved to be much more straightforward. Professor Wade, the major figure in Britain on constitutional law, agreed to help.

We raised with the prosecution the question of jury vetting and sought an assurance that since Roy Amlot had confirmed national security was not involved in this case there would be no vetting of the jury. After an exchange of correspondence we received an assurance from the Director of Public Prosecutions on 28 December that:

> The Prosecution itself cannot foresee the need to refer to any material which would require the court to go *in camera*.

They only asked that we should make the same assurance. This we were willing to do in general since we had nothing to hide and always wanted to hold the trial in open court. The main argument was over the 'Crown Jewels'. We wanted an expurgated version without highly classified information simply to establish that certain basic facts were known inside MOD.

By the middle of January agreement was still not possible and so we made an application to go before the Judge in Chambers in No. 2 Court at the Old Bailey. Bruce Laughland made a long speech outlining how we proposed to run the case and stating that we were not treating it as a party political trial. Roy Amlot made conciliatory noises and said that the expurgated version of the 'Crown Jewels' had been prepared as requested and only needed to be approved by Michael Heseltine. We left the Old Bailey feeling reasonably satisfied and expecting the issue to be resolved amicably.

Three days later, only ten days before the opening of the trial, there was a complete volte-face by the prosecution. Heseltine had looked at the expurgated 'Crown Jewels' and refused to release it. Instead it was decided that the full version, including the intelligence information, should be used. This meant the court would have to go *in camera* and the jury would be vetted. Jury vetting is normally only undertaken for terrorist or espionage trials. It involves Special Branch investigating every member of the jury panel. There is also a check on possible criminal records. The prosecution is then able to exclude those it dislikes. It was also taking a great risk with information vital to national security. The 'Crown Jewels' had been shown to half a dozen people in Whitehall. It was now to be given to twelve jurors and the lawyers and court officials. All of this in a desperate attempt to secure a conviction in a political trial. But we also had to face other last-minute obstacles. The prosecution produced statements from three new witnesses and in addition much of the evidence we had asked for from MOD was only provided the week before the start of the trial. We decided to dispute the need for jury vetting and on a Saturday morning five working days before the opening of the trial we went before the judge in his home in Pimlico to contest the actions by the prosecution so close to the date of the trial. We did not really expect to win, and we didn't.

The next day the *Observer* carried the story that the trial might be held *in camera*. Both *The Times* and the *Guardian* came out against vetting the jury. Many saw it as yet another example of political interference in the case. The DPP first denied that they had asked for the jury to be vetted, although requests were supposed to originate from them under the Attorney-General's guidelines published in 1980. Once again the issues were taken up in Parliament. David Steel, the Liberal leader, described the forthcoming trial as 'an East European-style secret trial'. Over fifty MPs signed an Early Day Motion protesting and for nearly ten minutes proceedings in the Commons were held up with points of order as Members protested about the vetting of the jury. The political atmosphere before the trial was certainly becoming red-hot. My local MP, Chris Smith, did much to help and in the week before the trial introduced a Ten-Minute Bill to abolish Section 2. This again helped focus the political debate.

In retrospect the whole period from my arrest to the start

of the trial seemed to have gone by in a flash. It was five months of hectic activity. I had never before been so busy, and writing this book had to be squeezed into odd moments in between work on preparing my defence. My time had largely been spent on research for the case, in legal conferences and making various detailed statements for my legal team and commenting on the prosecution evidence. It was also a time of uncertainty and tension and at the back of my mind I always had the prospect of up to two years in jail to consider. It was impossible to make any firm plans beyond the end of the trial. How would it all turn out? By the end of January we had our case ready, but we all recognised that this was not going to be an easy case to win. In the end it would depend on the composition of the jury, how they saw the case and how the case went from day to day and hour to hour in court. It was bound to be a difficult battle as we took on the power of the state in the courtroom.

CHAPTER SEVEN

DIARY OF A TRIAL

Day 1 (MONDAY 28 JANUARY)

This was bound to be a depressing day. We would just have to sit there and take it, while the Crown made out the best case they could with us virtually unable to say a word.

We breakfast at the Savoy, to boost our morale, then drive round to the Old Bailey and are shepherded in by the police. We have our own rooms for the duration of the trial. They call them the 'Jeremy Thorpe suite'. It's a room, a couple of toilets, some seedy tables and chairs all stamped *Domine Dirige Nos*, and a big security cabinet in which we are to keep our copies of the 'Crown Jewels' locked up at all times. But it is nice to have somewhere to come back to at lunchtime and eat our sandwiches in privacy.

When we arrive in No. 2 Court, I can see Tam Dalyell at the back. The DPP himself, Sir Thomas Hetherington, is in the Crown benches. Clearly he means to watch this case in person, all day. He, of course, reports directly to the Attorney-General.

They make me sit halfway down the stairs beneath the dock, and then come up when the judge arrives, to perch on a very uncomfortable chair.

First the jury is sworn in. Despite the ostentatious jury vetting, the Crown tell us none of them have shown up on Special Branch files, nor on criminal records. We intend to use the three challenges, which is all the defence are allowed: I take off three elderly middle class women. They are so clearly of a similar type that we fear they will form a little social group and all vote the same way.

First the jury is sworn in. Despite the ostentatious jury

vetting, the Crown tell us none of them have shown up on Special Branch files, nor on criminal records. We intend to use the three challenges, which is all the defence are allowed: I take off three elderly middle-class women. They are so clearly of a similar type that we fear they will form a little social group and all vote the same way.

Mr Justice McCowan flourishes a press release about Channel 4's proposed nightly half-hour reconstruction of the trial. We are in a peculiar position: we are not bothered whether they do the programme or not, but the last thing we want to do is give the impression the defence is behind the project. So when the judge says, 'I am greatly troubled by this ... actors will be taking the part of the participants, including the judge', we do not oppose his announcement that he will ban it. Later, Mark Carlisle QC and Geoffrey Robertson arrive representing Channel 4, and protest that the judge is exceeding his powers under the Contempt Act. The judge simply refuses to hear them. Channel 4 say they will go ahead with the programme, replacing actors with journalists.

Amlot starts a really boring opening speech, slogging his way through very slowly and precisely, reading out all the forty minutes and memoranda in the case. The jury must be completely baffled by this Whitehall prose.

They do sit up and pay attention though, when Bruce makes his formal admission that I did it. Perhaps they're wondering what on earth they're here for, if that's the case.

I have seen the draft of Amlot's opening speech over the weekend, so there is nothing to relieve the tedium.

'You may think that one of the questions in this case must be why he chose to leak documents to an MP who had been pursuing for some considerable time the particular line of inquiry Dalyell had? The Crown alleges the information he fed to Dalyell gives a misleading impression of the true position as known to Ponting.' He proceeds to attack my character during the police evidence, just as he had previously done at the committal: 'So, he did not tell the truth... it does look, does it not, as though he were saying someone else was responsible?'

I am relieved when Amlot makes the straightforward admission: 'It is not suggested that the disclosure in fact damaged national security.' But he goes on to the centrepiece – the 'Crown Jewels': 'We do not want to fight the Falklands War again. But the only way you can judge what it was Ponting disclosed is by comparing it with the position as known to him, which was embodied in the "Crown Jewels".' He goes on: 'This comparison will assist you greatly upon the question of whether he was acting in accordance with his duty in the interests of the State in making the disclosure he did.'

Bruce Laughland gets to his feet to fight the *in camera* application, quoting all the correspondence we had had with the DPP since 22 November before the dramatic reversal of course a week before the trial, and mentioning the 'undue drama' of calling the report the 'Crown Jewels'. 'Open justice should be done openly,' he says. He gets out one good line: 'It's not a case about spying. It's a case about lying, or misleading Parliament,' which catches the media attention next day.

Into camera we go, nonetheless. The glass windows in the doors are boarded up, and for twenty-five minutes the court is swept for bugging devices. From 3.25 to 4.20, Amlot wades through the text of the 'Crown Jewels', pointing to co-ordinates on a map, and reading out texts of intelligence material. I am not sure the jury are much the wiser. My only contribution to my trial all day has been to answer my name and plead 'Not guilty'.

We are now quite clear what our own tactics are. It has never been any part of our case that the Government was wrong to sink the *Belgrano*: they've stressed the issue precisely in order to take the jury's eye off the ball. Lying to Parliament will be the core and totality of our case.

We never thought, anyway, that this was going to be one of our best days...

Day 2 (TUESDAY 29 JANUARY)

Bruce manages to get me out of the dock – the judge agrees the case has 'special circumstances'. So I'm now on the solicitors' bench. Instead of having to sit up in the dock in silence, I can now talk to the others and discuss tactics.

The first prosecution witness is Richard Mottram, Heseltine's Private Secretary. I like Richard: we're about the same age and I've always thought we got on very well. He's pretty outspoken and cynical about it all, but rather enjoys Whitehall politics. Amlot leaves it to his junior, Tim Langdale, to take Richard's evidence. Langdale is another smooth, cold, flat operator.

We reach the 'Crown Jewels'. Once again, the court is cleared. I don't expect this to take very long, but we end up spending the whole day *in camera*. Langdale goes through the 'Crown Jewels' with Mottram literally line by line. They have an interminable technical dialogue, reading out the intelligence assessments while the jury look on, virtually ignored. After lunch, we agree that Bruce will intervene right away and cross-examine Richard. Then we can get the whole *in camera* session over and done with.

Bruce merely highlights the bits of the 'Crown Jewels' which we wish to emphasise. Richard isn't really being cross-examined: he is just having slightly different points drawn out of him. But he is a good bit more defensive than he was at the committal and seems to be defending the Ministerial line more strongly. Bruce puts some effort into appearing a slightly warmer sort of chap than those on the prosecution team.

All in all, another dull, tedious day.

Day 3 (WEDNESDAY 30 JANUARY)

When the session starts, Bruce makes a nice joke about the Channel 4 'reconstruction' being in the end 'not so much antiseptic as anaesthetic'. Then it is a long slog through the documents again. It is even less exciting than yesterday.

Richard Mottram faithfully follows Heseltine's 'national security' line: that the real decision was to limit disclosure 'before it touched on national security'. When he describes Stanley intervening to suppress my draft because it was 'inconsistent with the PM's own letter to Dalyell', Bruce gets up to protest: 'He is talking about the Minister's motives. No Minister is going to give evidence in this case.' We shall hammer home Ministerial failure to appear and explain themselves, whenever we can.

Bruce rises to cross-examine. This is the first time the public will hear anything of our case: he is going to try and show what all the Whitehall prose really means. Bruce raises the subject of Parliamentary Questions:

'It has long been the constitutional practice that the answer is a truthful one?'

'Yes.'

'And not deliberately ambiguous or misleading?'

A long pause. 'In highly-charged political matters, one person's ambiguity may be another person's truth.'

A good riposte – eventually. If Richard puts a foot wrong, he will face Heseltine's wrath.

Bruce makes some good points as the afternoon wears on. But it is tiring work. He quotes Stanley's memo about 'deep water', with another witty question (picked up by TV news that night): 'The depth of the water – not the *heat* of the water?'

Richard says gamely: 'Deep water from a security point of view: the questions are not a process which ends there.'

'Why not?' says Bruce sharply. 'It can end there. You could say, "Security does not permit me to answer a, b, or c." All these matters said to give rise to deep water have now been revealed without damage to the security of the state. No sailors' lives have been imperilled.'

The judge intervenes: 'Has that brought an end to public controversy – answering the questions he was asked?'

'Certainly not, my Lord,' Richard says, relieved. How thoughtful of the judge to help with his answers.

I thought we did quite well this afternoon. We're getting over to the jury that there is something else behind this.

Day 4 (THURSDAY 31 JANUARY)

A worrying incident. Two separate reports about our phones being tapped. Last night, someone rang my junior counsel, Jonathan Caplan, and invited himself round, saying he feared his phone was tapped. He heard we had complained to the judge about our own phone being tapped and 'wondered what reaction we had got'. We had not made any complaint. He came round to Jonathan's chambers and made him rather suspicious. It was an odd approach: was he some kind of stooge? Jonathan confided that several days ago he noticed his front door was opening much more easily, as though it had been tampered with in some way.

I would have dismissed this, but today Brian was approached out of the blue by a journalist. He said: 'I've got intelligence sources. They say there's a flap on over there, because your counsel's seeing the judge over his phone being bugged. My sources say it's to do with something that blew up last night.' We weren't planning to do anything of the kind, of course, but how did he get the same bit of information? Are our lines being tapped, or is some kind of set-up being manufactured? Bruce speaks to the judge, saying he wants an assurance: he is told the DPP, Sir Thomas Hetherington, will investigate personally. Sir Thomas is taking this case extraordinarly seriously: he is here in charge, all day, every day.

In court, the entrails of the Department continue to be spread out.

We had quite a good morning, bringing out the flavour of the 'Crown Jewels' meeting with Heseltine. Richard Mottram largely agreed with us in an open-minded sort of way, as Bruce cross-examined.

Goodness knows if we are making any headway with the jury, but they are listening to some extraordinary revelations about the real obsessions of this Government.

The case is taking shape. In the afternoon, my two subordinates from DS5, Margaret Aldred and Nick Darms, were hauled in to try and make out that the text of the Legge memorandum to the Foreign Affairs Committee had been somehow approved by me first – and was therefore part of my 'plot' to embarrass the Government.

It emerged quickly that little more than a passing chat was under discussion – a tiny event which neither could really remember, and which Inspector Broome had asked them to put together in identical statements, written jointly, not three weeks ago. Nobody could find a single document initialled by me. I felt sorry for their predicament.

Legge himself was now wheeled in, author of the famous memorandum. Bruce asked him: 'Were you troubled at all by the general nature of this letter...this somewhat disingenuous letter...you didn't take the view it was disingenuous?' Legge said, 'No.' But he does admit Ministers ended up by making public more information 'than they had wished to'.

A slightly odd day. I might find myself testifying tomorrow at this rate. My time in the witness-box may be the pivot of this trial: it will certainly be the most difficult part.

Day 5 (FRIDAY 1 FEBRUARY)

What a pompous so-and-so Richard Hastie-Smith is in the witness-box! Speaking out of the back of his throat, in his grey suit, he denies that any deal was struck with me. It is going to be a hard day. Hastie-Smith admits my resignation was 'one of the possibilities mentioned'. The questions remain as to why he accepted a resignation letter from me; and why he never suspended me on the spot. His explanation of the last is: 'It wasn't convenient,' he says, 'I was out of my office.'

'But we have been given the impression the MOD never sleeps,' Bruce says acidly. I like his jokes. He's on top form today, and his tone of voice is excellent. Then Bruce gets him on the ropes. How was it, he asks, that Hastie-Smith made a long formal statement stressing there was never any 'bargain', weeks before anyone had publicly claimed there was even a deal. 'Was it clairvoyance?' he demands. Hastie-Smith hesitates. Then the moment is ruined. Mr Justice McCowan decides he can't quite understand the point being

made, and his intervention gives Hastie-Smith a couple of
minutes to think about his answer.

I lean down and whisper to Brian Raymond: 'It feels like
having *two* prosecuting counsel against you.'

There is another good moment as Bruce goes through
Detective Chief Inspector Hughes' evidence. He is denying
everything very aggressively: 'I will never forget his
response... I will always remember that... I remember him
saying it distinctly.'

Bruce takes him to the point in his notes where I
supposedly collapse under his interrogation: 'A very, very
important psychological moment in interrogations, that's
when the conscientious and experienced police officer goes in
for the kill...?' Hughes is sagely assenting to the thrust of
this. 'So why did you then break off the questioning in order
to allow him to see his wife?'

Hughes in the end claims he was forced to let me see in
private my lawyer or my wife, at the moment the idea crossed
my mind.

Hughes' subordinate, Inspector Broome, cuts a miserable
figure, sunk in lugubriousness. Bruce quickly establishes the
informal way they were working – Hughes both interrogating
me and simultaneously scribbling the odd note. Even better
Hughes' 'contemporaneous notes' have a doodle in his own
hand of a sinking ship. Broome has an even more despondent
air when Bruce drags him up and down about his formal
witness statements. Broome's first statement omitted all
mention of my resignation letter, which he watched me write.
Then, only three weeks ago he makes another statement all
about it.

'You didn't think it was relevant when you drafted your
first statement on 31 August?' says Bruce sarcastically. 'Yet it
was relevant enough for you to put in your pocket book
beforehand.'

It's a real trial for once, these challenges and combats. But
that's it. The Crown case is suddenly all over, and the defence
calls its first witness, me. This is the moment of my – I
suppose 'ordeal' is the best word.

Last night, Bruce called me up. He said: 'Sleep well. The mass of the public out there are right behind you.' Then he said loudly over the phone: 'Goodnight, Sergeant Bloggs.'

Of course I'm nervous. I feel 'cold', in the theatrical sense taut and hoarse. Bruce has to remind me to speak up. We just go through my early life and career.

On Monday, the real test.

Day 6 (MONDAY 4 FEBRUARY)

I spent the weekend trying to relax. I was tired, and although Sally agreed things were less tense than we'd thought, you don't really forget what's happening. I'm trying to be philosophical: giving evidence, fighting this case, is something that's got to be done, so I'll do it as well as I can.

As soon as we arrive, there is a row about Tam Dalyell. He'd been sounding off in *The Times* and the *Guardian*, saying John Stanley falsified Sir John Fieldhouse's official despatch. This was pretty garbled. Amlot complained about it – I wonder why? Just as I am in the witness box trying to explain why I gave these papers to Dalyell, the judge hauls Dalyell in front of him in the well of the court: it is quite entertaining to see him spluttering about 'the high court of Parliament' and answering McCowan back. McCowan, misunderstanding when Tam said he'd only partially heard the judge's opening remarks (he came in half way through), proceeds to deliver the rest of his harangue very slowly and loudly as though to a deaf foreigner. McCowan threatens to put him in jail if he doesn't stop making speeches.

I give my whole account of the *Belgrano* affair, led along by Bruce with a nice balance of relaxation and occasional sharpness. The judge appears to be listening, and taking plenty of notes.

We are trying to meet the Crown's theory that I acted out of pique because my proposals were chopped down, and trying to get across that I am a normal civil servant. You don't exactly re-live the experience of the cover up, testifying up here from this vantage-point in the witness-box. The exercise is too controlled for that, as you try and keep a clear perspective on events. It's hard work: I've got to concentrate all the time and not dare relax for a second.

'I wasn't prepared to keep my mouth shut,' I say. 'It was an issue of principle. Somebody, somehow, had to tell Parliament.' I imagined, this afternoon, when I got on to this part, that the Court seemed appreciably hushed – I've talked it all through so many times that I no longer have any idea how the whole affair strikes ordinary people.

I'll be on again tomorrow, when I'll spell out the deal made with the police and Hastie-Smith. And then, Amlot will cross-examine me. Everyone says he's not to be under-estimated: and I suppose his whole aim will be to discredit me somehow. Sir Thomas Hetherington, the DPP, spent all day in court *again*.

Day 7 (TUESDAY 5 FEBRUARY)

After Bruce had taken me through the 'deal' with the Department, Amlot batters me under cross-examination for the rest of the day. It's not as if you get any audience reaction: I don't know whether this is a 'stiff' cross-examination or not. (Later people said it was.) But I feel I am not giving way on any points of substance, and sometimes turn round and hit his questions back at him. It's pure politics! Amlot barely took a single note while I was giving my evidence, and stands up, with the DPP behind his back once again, to present what is plainly a fixed 'line'. He is counsel for Havers and Heseltine and his instructions are clearly to take a purely political position.

Of course, he'd love me to say it was all a conspiracy to scupper Peru. I think they really imagined we would say that. I emphasise that everything was done on the basis of the intelligence assessments, and I point out as sharply as I can that I never saw all the 'Peru' material – the Foreign Office just sent across to me a few telegrams which appeared to back up the PM's position.

Bruce stands up at one point and protests unavailingly: 'Mr Amlot is not counsel for Mrs Thatcher and the War

Cabinet.' But Amlot plods on to the next brick in his pile – the Dalyell connection. This boils down to saying: 'Dalyell was a critic of the Government' – as though this made his activities quite illegitimate.

Then Amlot goes for blood. 'These facts you leaked would have been marvellous ammunition for Dalyell and the other critics.'

He repeats this accusation again and again. Each time I explain, as stoutly as I can: 'I do not believe it was ammunition. It was material which shows the Government's explanations to Parliament were not truthful.'

Amlot goes on flinging this phrase 'marvellous ammunition'. I say: 'If the decision to sink the *Belgrano* was correct, then it was correct to tell the truth to Parliament.'

He demands to know how I imagined Dalyell 'of all people' would react to the leaks: 'I don't know why you say "of all people". Dalyell is a duly elected MP, with the same rights and responsibilities as any other Member of Parliament.'

The next line of attack was the 'slippery slope' theory about national security. Wouldn't these disclosures simply egg Dalyell on to ask appalling questions about top-secret intelligence matters? I say the Government had spent the previous two years saying there were secret intelligence 'indications' of an attack, and brushing off those who pressed for details. What was novel? As we come up to lunch, I riposte: 'At the end of the day, at some point, because intelligence may be involved, it doesn't mean no questions can be answered about a particular subject.'

I say there was only one 'line' – between classified and unclassified information. 'I'm bound to say I've never heard that slippery slope argument inside MOD, and it was not used until after the disclosures in autumn... what was discussed at length were the political difficulties.'

'The decision the Secretary of State made to draw the line was based on sound sensible grounds?'

'No, it was not. It was based on political considerations.'

'You must accept the vital questions had to be declined on grounds of intelligence.'

'The vital questions were being declined on grounds of political embarrassment.'

By the middle of the afternoon Amlot and I are really slogging it out. Amlot makes a huge play with the fact that the key phrase in the Legge minute had, as he put it, 'originated within your own department'. I say it had been news to me until I saw the prosecution evidence last month.

Whenever Amlot rummaged around in his papers, I expected him to produce some terrific *coup de theatre*. But none came.

There are some good moments in the afternoon. Amlot quotes one of Dalyell's letters accusing Heseltine of 'post-facto rationalisation' about national security. Taking my opportunity, I say: 'A very elegant phrase – and not too far from the truth.' As the afternoon ends, Amlot says in his slowest and most menacing tone: 'Do you still say you did this from high motives?' Rather hoarsely, I say: 'Yes.' To my astonishment, he slowly sits down. The cross-examination is over.

Day 8 (WEDNESDAY 6 FEBRUARY)

We are all looking forward to a good day. But by the end we felt that it was the day when the trial seems to have been decided against us. Bruce re-examines me and sends down full tosses which I hit to the boundary. Mrs Thatcher's final letter to George Foulkes is read out, in which she publicly admits every one of the facts which I am being tried for leaking – and a few more besides. Amlot leaps up and waves about a copy of the *New Statesman*, saying Foulkes only took up the issue when the leaked documents were reproduced there. He demands Bruce read it into the record. Bruce is sarcastic: 'What do you want me to read? There's an article in here headed 'Why the *Belgrano* papers matter' – or here's another one called, 'Lies, Damned Lies and Answers to Tam Dalyell'. There is, as they say, laughter in court.

The jury are taking a definite interest. They pass up a note demanding to be supplied with a) the copy of the *New Statesman* b) copies of the Gavshon and Rice book *The*

Sinking of the Belgrano and c) Chief Inspector Hughes'
'contemporaneous notes'. They get the *New Statesman* and
are refused the others.

Then the judge asks me questions. It's like a second cross-
examination for the prosecution. 'Were you not prepared to
confess to the police, unless there was no prosecution? . . .
Did you think at the time you had a defence under the Official
Secrets Act? . . . Why then did you not say so in your written
statement?'

My junior counsel, Jonathan Caplan, puts in a statement
from Lord Rayner. He speaks of my 'strength of character'
during the 1979 efficiency studies and says: 'He handled this
difficult task with distinction.'

He is followed by our constitutional expert, Professor
Henry Wade, Master of Gonville & Caius, Cambridge. Wade
explains that constitutional 'conventions' are the fundamental rules of British political life, without which 'relations
between Government and Parliament would all go awry'. He
adds: 'The conventions could not exist unless Ministers gave
truthful answers to Parliament.'

But when Jonathan gets to the point, McCowan promptly
intervenes. McCowan says: 'This is for me to decide. It may
be a matter of law. The jury has to accept my direction on the
law.'

After much argument with Jonathan, he finally allows
Wade to go on. But he ostentatiously makes no notes.

And now – our star witness, Merlyn Rees. The judge is, I
expect, none too pleased to see him. It is important that we
have a senior ex-Minister to give evidence. The prosecution
could not produce one Minister to defend their policies.
Merlyn says: 'If I'd thought there'd been a breach of security,
I would not have come along this morning.'

He talks about his war record, his time in Northern Ireland
and his Home Secretaryship, when he was in charge of MI5.
'Since that time,' Merlyn says gravely, 'I have had police
protection. A Minister is responsible to Parliament . . . Just
after the Falklands War, when Humphrey Atkins inadvertently gave false information, he came and corrected it

immediately. It matters to tell the truth.'

On my own case, Merlyn comes up to scratch: 'Loyalty to a Minister and a Government must be there, but the loyalty to his nation is greater. If a civil servant found himself with a crisis of conscience, and no channels offering reasonable prospect of redress, should he simply resign and say nothing? If those were the circumstances, I would put truthfulness to Parliament above all. A member of MI5 used to brief Winston Churchill in the 30s: he thought it was his duty then . . .'

In cross-examination Amlot tries to persuade him these disclosure decisions are all to do with national security, and depend on the judgement of the Minister. 'If he considers they are of a security nature, yes, but not if it is to the political embarrassment of the Government.'

And in comes Sally, our final witness. The judge is gratuitously rude to her, snapping at her to speak up, and halting her on grounds of 'hearsay'. He knows, I suppose, that she will corroborate my story of the deal, as she does.

Around lunchtime the bombshell came. Amlot and the DPP have not only put in submissions trying to rule out *mens rea*, they are also submitting that 'interests of the State' – which is the fundamental pillar of our defence – must have an impossibly narrow meaning. They argue that it is the same thing as 'Government policy', ie that the interests of the State consist of the political interests of Michael Heseltine. It seems such a ludicrous and undemocratic proposition that although we are worried we cannot believe the judge could accept such an argument.

Then McCowan, having sent the jury home for the afternoon, announces: 'These draft submissions go to very crucial arguments. If the prosecution submissions are right, I will have to direct the jury to convict.' He can't be serious.

But it turns out he is. Jonathan Caplan's arguments all get short shrift. 'Duty' in the statute does not merely mean 'official duty', Jonathan argues it could include contractual, moral, or civic duty. Mr Justice McCowan: 'Any old duty will do?'

On *mens rea* the judge deals with the conflicting views of Caulfield in the Aitken case of 1971, and Mars-Jones in the 'ABC' case of 1978, by demanding: 'What if secrets were handed over to a foreign power because a civil servant honestly thought we'd all be much better off as a result?' He ignores Jonathan's point that that sort of situation has nothing to do with Section 2, and is a classic espionage Section 1 matter.

On the crucial question of 'interests of the State', Jonathan quotes two Law Lords in the crucial case from the early 1960s. Lord Reid said: 'State is not an easy word. It does not mean the Government or the Executive . . . the interests of the majority are not the same as the interests of the State.' Reid talks about 'the realm' and the 'organised community' and on the issue of the public interest, says: 'Governments or Ministers do not as a general rule have the last word about that.'

McCowan remarks facetiously: 'He's your high spot, isn't he? . . .'

Jonathan presses on: 'The Crown must satisfy the jury. Mr Ponting was not under a duty to do what he did. Even if the jury were to return a perverse verdict, that is their prerogative.'

McCowan shows growing enthusiasm for ordering the jury to convict me: 'If the Crown's right, there isn't any scope for an acquittal . . . he was clearly not acting "in the interests of the State" in a narrow way. He was not acting in the interests of the Government.'

But Amlot starts at this point to behave in a very strange fashion. At the moment of his apparent triumph, he shows signs of alarm: 'There must be some material for the jury to consider. The Crown would be very reluctant to persuade you to direct the jury to convict.'

McCowan is undeterred: 'What is the material for the jury? . . .'

Amlot continues to back-pedal: 'You have to look at the policy of the Secretary of State to see whether it should be disclosed or not . . .' He suddenly asks for an overnight adjournment. But McCowan sails on: 'If the evidence is all one way, where is the evidence to justify a finding of not guilty? It clearly wasn't in the interests of the Government to disclose the material...'

Amlot becomes so flustered, he makes a most un-characteristic slip, and comes out with the truth. 'I am very reluctant that in this of all cases you should finish up directing the jury to convict!'

So that's what he means! I lean across and whisper to Brian: 'And they say they don't have political trials in this country!' It was like watching the scenery suddenly slip at an opera, and men running across the stage.

Amlot scribbles a note to the DPP behind him. Sir Thomas strides hastily out of the court. I wonder who he went to telephone? What a grossly political trial! Then Amlot demands an adjournment, if only for ten minutes. The judge disappears from public view. When he returns and Amlot resumes his place, everything has altered. Amlot stands up and says formally: 'Even if your ruling is in our favour, we do not ask for a direction to convict.' The judge announces that someone has just shown him another case which has made him change his mind entirely on the law. He was wrong before.

The judge is probably going to tell the jury that the 'interests of the State' are the same as the political interests of Michael Heseltine. On that basis there is no way we can win. All we can do is wait and see what the outcome is supposed to be. Is it prison or is it something less? Just what sort of trial is this supposed to be? David Steel said a week before the start that it was 'an East European-style secret trial' – it looks as though he was right.

Day 9 (THURSDAY 7 FEBRUARY)

This morning, exactly as predicted, the judge ruled out *mens rea* as a defence. He went on, again as predicted, to define 'interests of the State' as 'the policies of the organs of government'. So our whole defence has been swept away. The Crown have got the jury going out to consider a verdict –

but it's a jury left with no practical option but to convict. Their task has become a charade; McCowan summons the twelve members of the jury back in. 'Counsels' speeches will now be geared to my rulings,' he informs them. 'They have to accept my rulings in law, just as *you* do.'

Amlot opens his prosecution final speech by rubbing in his victory. 'Interests of the State' does not mean some wide and all-embracing public interest,' he says. He then proceeds to assert that the 'broader' interest of the state is to keep official information secret. 'It's not just the law – it's good sense. It has applied in this country for centuries now. Heseltine made it abundantly clear he was not prepared to go further and disclose information to Dalyell or anyone else ... How can any civilised country operate without that process of policy-making being treated in confidence? Leaks are bound to undermine the process of Government.'

To my astonishment, Amlot now launches into a political speech defending the sinking of the *Belgrano*. I thought all this had been ruled out as irrelevant. 'There is nothing sinister in the sinking of the *Belgrano* ... this is important when you come to consider whether Parliament has been misled or to what extent. You know, and very few people in this nation do, just how vital intelligence was.'

I thought it was supposed to be me on trial, not the War Cabinet.

Amlot reiterates his original instructions: the facts fed to Dalyell were misleading without the intelligence context; all the bogus Parliamentary answers over the years were purely designed to protect intelligence.

His next thesis is to prove I am involved in a plot. The facts I gave to Dalyell would have been 'music to his ears', and given him the 'clear impression there was a cover up', he says indignantly. He sticks to his brief that all the 'errors' about the *Belgrano* were accidental, and eventually rectified. Therefore, in this rather unlikely logic: 'What Ponting did in disclosing the information as he did, was not out of high motive because he felt Ministers were misleading the House. The real reason – I cannot give you. But you may wonder about the fact that the advice of others had been preferred on two occasions. It may have been out of pique or rancour . . . It is a simple issue. The Crown has to prove the case. But nobody is suggesting this is intended as some sort of test case, or to determine the relationships between civil servants and Ministers.'

After lunch, Bruce gets to his feet. His speech, constrained and crippled as it is by the judge's legal rulings, is our only chance of getting through to the jury.

He starts out being nice to them, saying self-deprecatingly that counsels' speeches rarely make much difference to the outcome and that modern juries are too sophisticated to endure windy rhetoric from barristers without being able to answer back. 'If you don't know the real issue by now, I have failed . . . we have built up before you, brick by brick, the defence of Clive Ponting. You should be able to see the substance of it by now, perfectly clearly. This is a hard and serious struggle: an individual citizen has taken action which has brought down on his head the whole apparatus of state. He has had the temerity to challenge the conduct of very senior and powerful Ministers.

'This case is unique in many ways: it is important to Clive Ponting; it may be of public importance – and the Government itself may even spare time to take an interest in its outcome! Barristers are not allowed to express their own opinions – they have to dress it up. But I'm going to break this rule in a small way, because I have one or two prejudices or biasses which I think we all share.

'The first is a strong prejudice in favour of the administration of justice according to the law. Section 2 of the Official Secrets Act has been the most criticised piece of legislation on the statute book. The judge is going to have the not entirely easy task of explaining what it means.

'. . . Pay heed, as you should do, to the voices of your conscience. Your oath is to return a "true" verdict. Be satisfied the verdict is a just one, according to the law.

'My second piece of bias is this: and it is not "soft-soaping" you. It is a prejudice in favour of the role of juries, particularly where the liberty of the subject is at stake. Lawyers, like politicians, don't always know best . . . see the truth with a seeing eye. Your verdict will have the special authority which no judge can aspire to: in this criminal matter, you speak as representatives of the public, and the public interest.

'This Act, passed in one afternoon, all that time ago, foresaw exceptional circumstances. Could they have been the situation Merlyn Rees touched on, when serving officers communicated to a member of the Parliamentary awkward squad – Winston Churchill – about our military unprepared-ness?

'The judge will give you help on the law. He will direct you on the "interests of the State". It would be unlikely if he were to suggest to you that the State was the same as the Conservative party, or that the State was embodied in the personage of Ministers! The security of the state is not the same as the security and safety of Ministers. Protecting the state from security disclosures is wholly different from protecting Ministers from political disclosures.

'The "organs of government", we say, include Parliament. Indeed Parliament is one of the supreme organs of government. We hope the individual policy of any British Government will always be to observe the principles and spirit of Parliamentary democracy. That must include the observing of the established rules and conventions. You all hope any Government has among its policies telling the truth to Parliament. You don't need me to point out it cannot do that if it's misled, or if even non-classified, relevant information is withheld – if it's fobbed off with some kind of security answer when it isn't a genuine security question. If so, democracy would be quickly lost. And that would be the real "slippery slope".

'The true nature of our defence has been known for a long time – since 10 August in fact, when Mr Ponting set out in ringing language, the contention he has consistently pursued:

"Ministers were seeking to avoid answering legitimate questions from MPs, in order to protect their own political position."

'Where are the invisible men? Where are the Ministers whose actions have been called into question? We know Mr Heseltine has an onerous and busy life. We read about it from time to time... We are sure that Mr Stanley has grave responsibilities...

'But if you are to be persuaded that what was done by the Department was not to save face, but for genuine reasons of national security – then couldn't the Ministers have spared half an hour to come down here and tell you about it?

'Hardly the Falklands Spirit. You might think, listening to Mr Amlot's speech, that it was the Ministers themselves who were on trial. He sounded as if he were defending them. We called someone with ministerial experience to testify.

'It may very well be that Mr Ponting has broken the Civil Service regulations: the house rules. If you think he has merely done that, well it doesn't involve the Official Secrets Act, and land you in the dock at the Central Criminal Court!

'The sinking of the cruiser *Belgrano* was a matter of undoubted public concern. And not just from Tam Dalyell alone. He wasn't a one-man band: there were others. Mr Ponting at least twice went on record advocating greater openness. Sir Clive Whitmore, the Permanent Under-Secretary, was in favour of greater openness too. It was Mr Stanley, we see, who decided it was more desirable to bring down the shutters... This is a unique case. The appearance or absence of motive is sometimes a touchstone for a jury. No-one suggests this was done for money. No-one suggests it was done for revenge. No-one suggests it was done to achieve some political end. The only other possible motive Mr Amlot can come up with – racking his brains – is pique! Absurd!'

By now, in Bruce Laughland's speech on my behalf, he was quite carefully watching the clock. Even at the risk of boring the jury, he was planning to spin it out to last until the end of the afternoon. The last thing we wanted was for the judge to speak for the last few minutes. At least this way the jury would have one night to sleep on what we had said and digest it, before what I feared was about to be a second prosecution speech – from the judge. So he started on a rather less pro-Government version of history.

After the sinking, said Bruce, Nott made his famous statement to the Commons. 'Thereafter there began a very strange process, which cannot have been attributable entirely to error. We say there was a developing policy to conceal by various means the real truth from the British public. It was not so much a Watergate – as an Underwatergate! There was a reluctance to reveal information amounting almost to a rearguard action on the part of the Government.

'I don't advance some theory of Government conspiracy. Some say it was errors, muddle, politicians and civil servants closing ranks. Remember Mr Mottram: – "Changing an account is always a difficult thing." Does that throw any light on the case?'

Bruce trawled once again through the untruths. And then on the Official Despatch: 'Did the MOD alter it? And if so, why? Or was the Admiral careless? You wouldn't expect the Senior Service to be that careless – it's about as unthinkable as that they should lose a navigational log!' I could see several members of the jury very visibly laughing.

Bruce speeds up now, and charges through the rest of the evidence. 'Dalyell may have been a thorn in the Government's side, but he was a specialist ... the worrying thing about Dalyell is that, although he took a lonely road, and had some contentious views – he's been right, right, and right again! ... Had Clive Ponting been the kind of person only intent on saving his own skin, he would never have had any crisis of conscience. Had he resigned first and then communicated the information – that would still have been an Official Secrets Act offence.

'The police make the prejudicial suggestion Mr Ponting was obliquely trying to blame his subordinates. That's not the man you saw in the dock. Whatever else he is, is he a liar? Judge the quality of his evidence.'

That's virtually it. Approaching 4.15 pm, and our last chance to plead my case. Bruce has only got his finale left:

'Mr Ponting presents a somewhat lonely, serious, and intelligent figure. But he is not asking for sympathy. Nor is he pretending he repents, despite the consequences so far. He was faced with an obligation to do his duty – in the true interests of the State – from which he did not shrink.

'If what he did was a crime, you know this could be a licence for Ministers to withhold information from the House of Commons, with the tame acquiescence of their civil servants: and so, infringe your liberties.

'If what he did was a crime in English Law, you say so. But if it is God help us – because no Government will!'

Day 10 (FRIDAY 8 FEBRUARY)
The Old Bailey trial has lasted now for two weeks and it's a strain. During Amlot's speech yesterday, I tried to distance myself, and look impassive in front of the jury.

Bruce's speech was good. But after that ruling by the judge, where does it leave us, except fighting hopelessly on? What the judge has ruled is the kind of thing the defendants pleaded at Nuremberg.

Before the start today we decided that our one hope would be for the judge to go over the top in his summing up and alienate the jury. We are not mistaken.

'The defence accept the evidence is all one way, that he was not authorised to make the disclosures. There is only one ingredient in dispute: "duty in the interests of the State".

'Duty, I direct you, means an official duty, namely that of an Assistant Secretary in the MOD. The Prosecution say "Where is there a scintilla of evidence it was his official duty?" It is plain his duty was to preserve these documents.

'Interest of the State, I direct you, means the policies of the State as they were in July 1984 when he communicated the documents, and not the policies as Ponting, Tam Dalyell, or any of us, think they ought to have been – the policies laid down for it by the recognised organs of Government and authority.

'We have General Elections in this country. The majority party in the House of Commons forms the Government. If it loses majority support, it ceases to do so, but for the time being, it *is* the Government, and its policies are those of the State.

'It is not a question of the Conservative party being the State. It is not a political matter at all. The policies of the State were the policies of the Government then in power. It is not in dispute that Government policy, rightly or wrongly, was not to give information. Ponting said: "This is Government policy – and I don't like it!" It cannot be in the interests of the State to have leaked these documents to Dalyell. What evidence is there against that?'

What is interesting is that while the judge is saying this, I can see at least one juror on the front row vigorously shaking his head.

McCowan proceeded to hammer in the nails. 'You are not concerned with whether you agree with the policies of the Government at that time...you are not concerned with whether the defendant honestly believed it was his duty to do what he did.

'You may be beginning to say to yourselves: "We have been treated for days to a great deal of irrelevant material". So you have.'

On we go, down this hopeless road: 'It is not necessary that the disclosure should have breached national security...this Act has been a great deal criticised. Governments are always saying they are going to do something about it, but they never do. Maybe it suits all Governments to keep it as it is... you are not concerned in this case with whether the Act needs repeal or amendment.

'You may have noted Mr Laughland's final remarks to you... I say emphatically this would be a wholly wrong approach to your duties and oath. If the case is proved, it is your duty to convict, whatever the consequences... the political consequences of convicting or acquitting are not a matter for you.'

Mr Justice McCowan is in full flood by now: 'There are a

lot of other things this case is not about ... not about which country has the better right to the Falklands, not about whether the war could have been avoided; not about whether the Fortress Falklands policy is a good idea ... not about whether Clive Ponting was wiser than Mr Heseltine. Mr Stanley and Mr Heseltine thought otherwise ... It was a political decision, but Mr Ponting thought he knew better.

'Civil servants must bear with fortitude having their advice not followed, even if they think themselves infinitely wiser and more intelligent than Ministers. It is not the point.

'Nor is it a political contest. It is your duty to put your political allegiances or prejudices on one side. Any Government has to face the problem about what to reveal to the public, and has to expect from its civil servants' loyalty – that they will not leak to the Opposition. That is a comment – it is entirely a matter for you.'

This was to be the first of many such comments. 'Don't let sympathy sway you,' McCowan is urging, as I try to endure this catalogue. 'Sympathy for his comparative youth, his promise, his lost career.' Having finished his task of virtually directing the jury to convict, he embarks on what he calls 'a historical summary'. This consists of a speech backing the Government for sinking the *Belgrano*. But then he proceeds to conduct himself in a way which makes me lean over to Brian and whisper, 'It sounds like a speech at the Tory party conference.'

On the Fieldhouse Despatch row he says: 'No-one was suggesting Ministers were involved. No-one was suggesting a deliberate lie had been told.'

By lunchtime Bruce says: 'I've counted three grounds of appeal already so far.' After lunch the judge continues vigorously down the same road. Going through all the documents yet again, he manages to omit most of what the defence say about them.

McCowan spends an extraordinary amount of time telling the jury how important is the Darms/Aldred evidence (which the prosecution claimed showed that I had agreed the crucial parts of the Legge Minute), pursuing a thesis he finds enormously attractive, that I deliberately invented ministerial policy towards the Foreign Affairs Committee, in order to get Heseltine and Stanley into trouble. What about my side of the story?

He cheerfully quotes Mottram's hearsay evidence: 'Mr Stanley believed Heseltine would get into deep water from a security point of view... Do you accept Mr Mottram as an honest and accurate witness of ministerial thinking at that time?'

Then he quotes Heseltine's 'slippery slope' testimony to the Foreign Affairs Committee in November, as though this clinches the issue of what Heseltine might have been thinking in April. The judge then freely embroiders my imaginary motives, without a shred of evidence – 'Pique' he says, 'spite, wounded pride...' He hints that 'interests of the State' was merely a late excuse I dreamed up for my conduct. Hastie-Smith's evidence is handled reverently; that everything was done to prosecute me as a matter of normal, formal, routine: 'Ponting knew of legal matters: he would have had some knowledge of the laid-down course. Sir Ewan Broadbent knew the Minister would have to be told – wouldn't it be likely the laid-down course would be followed?'

And then – why didn't I express some visible outrage, if the deal had really been reneged on? 'One might have expected some reaction of distinct anger; some sort of protest.'

Naturally he takes the side of the policemen: 'You saw Chief Inspector Hughes and Inspector Broome. Have they invented it? For what reason?' He never wonders what conceivable reason I could have had for manufacturing an elaborate story about being offered a deal. Why on earth should I make up something like that? He goes through the challenged parts of the police evidence with an air of faint incredulity that I should dispute so much – he reads out great chunks which are so wrong Bruce can contain himself no longer and leaps to his feet to protest. Bruce is getting really upset by the whole performance. McCowan has to admit he is reading out the wrong parts.

'If you think Hughes and Broome were tricking Ponting

into a confession, and inventing parts of it to discredit him – if you think that may have happened, you will not shrink from casting their evidence on one side.'

The judge then takes my evidence by reading it out selectively, saying 'it is my duty' to read it out (as though it were a distasteful one). He lards it with 'Mr Hughes totally denies that . . . You will recall Hastie-Smith totally denies this version.'

'You heard he had become a Buddhist. I'm sure none of you will hold it against him because he had changed his faith!'

It is easy to get angry with a hostile summing up. All I need to record really is that Professor Wade and Merlyn Rees were dealt with contemptuously, with no attempt to present the defence line of argument at all fairly. I did get upset with what he said about Sally's evidence: 'I'm sure we can all have sympathy with her, having to give evidence in these worrying circumstances.' It will probably look unexceptionable in the appeal transcript, but the mock-sympathy hid a pretty obvious innuendo.

Day 11 (MONDAY 11 FEBRUARY)

I think this weekend was the worst of all. I'm tired and dispirited after the judge's behaviour. My spirits were lifted by thinking of the scores of letters of support – and only three hostile ones.

The *Observer* printed the episode in the absence of the jury that was probably the turning-point of the trial. No-one else had published a word, assuming it to be contempt of court. David Leigh of the *Observer* says he has got strong legal advice that backs him. This article was a real turning point. Now the public would know exactly what had happened.

In court on Monday morning, McCowan makes a final assault on the jury's sensibilities by placing them *in camera* with all the mumbo-jumbo again, and ramming the 'Crown Jewels' down their throats.

'You may think that the sight of the 'Crown Jewels' has helped you greatly to get at the truth about the sinking of the *Belgrano*.' Then there comes the final smear. The *New*

Statesman is produced and read at enormous length: 'As a highly-intelligent and politically-conscious man, Ponting must have expected what would be written by strong critics of the Government.' He does not say that not a word from any of these documents appeared in print anywhere until my arrest provoked Dalyell into outrage. 'Spite . . . no defence he honestly believed it was his duty . . . political debate outside the range of your discussions . . . the policies of the Government included as a matter of fact that the line should be drawn where Mr Heseltine drew it. You are not concerned with whether it was a wise decision. There it is.'

He sends the jury out.

After a brief exchange about the *Observer* article we leave the court and retire to the 'Jeremy Thorpe suite' to await the verdict. We had breakfasted at the Savoy again, but I had little appetite. My pockets were full of stuff for prison where I expected to be in a few hours' time. Most of the time we pace up and down the room discussing grounds of appeal, how we could not accept the judge's ruling on 'interests of the State' and how we would fight on to the European Court of Human Rights.

We try to eat some lunch but everybody is tense and despondent, though trying to be cheerful.

Suddenly at 2 pm the jury bailiff comes in saying, 'Mr Ponting, please come into court immediately, we have a verdict.' I just had time to kiss Sally goodbye. I try to keep my mind a blank as I go into the dock and down the stairs to sit on the chair facing the cells, wondering if I will be going down there in a few minutes. After the judge comes in I go up the steps and stand at the front of the dock in an absolutely packed court. The clerk of the court stands up and asks the jury foreman, a young, bearded man who is smiling, whether they have reached a verdict. 'Yes.'

'And is it the verdict of you all?'

'Yes.'

The clerk reads out the charge and then says, 'Do you find the defendant Guilty or Not Guilty?'

'Not Guilty,' is the reply. There is an audible gasp in court followed by cheering and clapping. I gasp too and smile at Sally. Bruce has the presence of mind to ask for our costs which are granted.

I leave the dock and run from the court to embrace Sally. It has hardly sunk in – what an historic verdict, and unanimous too. We are all so elated we can hardly talk when we get back to our room. The first decision is to celebrate that night with everybody who has helped. We book a restaurant and then leave the Old Bailey through a cheering crowd to ITN for an interview and champagne. After a brief rest in a hotel where the time is spent phoning friends I have to appear live on Channel 4 news, dodge the photographers and cameras and join the celebrations at the Soho restaurant. A wonderful evening with everybody ecstatic that we have pulled off a fantastic win. Thank God for the jury. A visit to 'Newsnight' on BBC2, then back to the party and finally home at 2 am.

An incredible day that started in the depths has ended on the heights. The implications have not sunk in but the celebrations were marvellous. We have won a tremendous victory and the jury has made an historic decision in favour of democracy.

HOUSE OF COMMONS
18 FEBRUARY 1985

Exactly a week after my unanimous acquittal the House of Commons held a major debate on the 'Sinking of the *General Belgrano*'. In his opening speech Michael Heseltine spent hardly any time on the decisions made in April and May 1982 and the subsequent cover up, but chose to spend nearly all of his hour-long speech in a personal attack on me. It was rather like Roy Amlot's closing speech for the prosecution at the trial. Heseltine was, of course, protected by Parliamentary privilege and not subject to cross-examination about what he said.

All of this was in marked contrast to his failure to appear at the Old Bailey and give evidence on oath at my trial about his actions; actions which were at the centre of the case. During his speech Michael Heseltine, when questioned about his failure to appear, said: 'If it had been considered necessary or desirable by those conducting the case to have called me to the court, I should, of course, have been prepared to go. They did not ask me to go or consult me about whether they should ask me to go, and I was not called.' This statement ignores the fact that at the committal proceedings on 9 October 1984, nearly four months before the trial, my junior counsel, Jonathan Caplan, specifically asked, in public, that Michael Heseltine should be called as he was a highly relevant witness. We never received any answer to this request.

During the debate Heseltine also placed some internal MOD documents in the Library of the House of Commons. This was a highly selective sample of the relevant documents, and only about one-quarter of all the documentation available at the trial (and read out in open court). The selection of documents, not unexpectedly, left out all the minutes of dissent I had written in the spring of 1984. The bundle of documents also contained some interesting additions. First, a minute recording decisions taken on 30 March which was never produced in court. Indeed we were told that no records of the 30 March meeting existed. Second, my initial draft reply to Tam Dalyell attached to the 'Crown Jewels' was included with the bundle. During the trial we were refused permission to detach and use some of the documents attached to the 'Crown Jewels' in open court. Had we been able to do this the minute from Francis Pym of 1 May 1982 could have been read out to the public showing the dissent within the War Cabinet. Obviously there was one rule in court and another when it was politically convenient to reveal information in Parliament.

In his speech Heseltine made a number of accusations about my behaviour that are neither internally consistent nor consistent with the full documentation available in court. I do not propose to refute here every single one of the points he made and I would simply refer the reader to Chapter 5 'The Battle for the Truth' which gives a full account of events inside MOD in the spring and early summer of 1984. There are however some general points worth making.

1. Before the 'Crown Jewels' were written, and before I arrived in DS5, John Stanley asked for two drafts to be prepared to answer the letter of 6 March to the Prime Minister from Denzil Davies. One of the drafts was to give the true date of detection and sighting of the *General Belgrano* by *HMS Conqueror*, the other would give the incorrect date of 2 May. The idea behind this exercise was to enable Ministers to choose which draft they wished to send. As I said at the time the information giving the correct date was unclassified and so the choice between the two drafts was essentially political. In other words Ministers had to choose whether to tell the truth.

2. Heseltine did make two specific charges against me. First, that I changed my advice for no reason and never made the position clear to Ministers. Second, that I urged Dalyell to keep going whilst telling Ministers not to release information. Neither charge is true or consistent with the documents. The 'Crown Jewels' were written in five days. The time for analysis was short. The initial draft reply to Tam Dalyell's letter attached to the 'Crown Jewels' could not be cleared with the intelligence staff in the time before it had to be sent to Heseltine. It was therefore a cautious reply not giving away information. At the meeting on 30 March with Heseltine, it was agreed that only one question in Tam Dalyell's letter would have to be declined on security grounds.

The day the Prime Minister replied to Denzil Davies (4 April) I circulated a new draft reply to Tam Dalyell answering his questions. This was agreed by the Royal Navy and the intelligence staff as unclassified.

I sent the reply to Heseltine on 12 April and it was rejected, on John Stanley's advice. On 18 April Heseltine sent a reply to Dalyell that was a simple refusal to answer any more questions even though the information was unclassified. Heseltine was fully aware of the unclassified nature of the material when he decided not to answer Dalyell's questions. It was a week later, when it was clear that Ministers had decided to continue the cover up that I wrote an anonymous note to Dalyell to tell him to keep going and to try and get at the truth.

Dalyell wrote to Heseltine again on 1 May and on 9 May I wrote another minute to Heseltine urging Ministers to come clean and tell the truth. I pointed out that the information was not classified and that there was no legitimate reason for withholding it. Again on John Stanley's advice he refused. When Dalyell wrote a third time in late May Heseltine no longer bothered to ask for my advice and his office wrote another brush-off reply.

3. Heseltine tried to imply in his speech on 18 February that I was involved in the preparation of the 'Legge Minute' which I later sent to Tam Dalyell to show how Ministers were misleading the Foreign Affairs Committee. This is not correct and although some of my staff were consulted by one of Michael Legge's staff the first time I saw this material was in January 1985 just before my trial. The minute was, anyway, faithfully carrying out Ministerial policy on how to deal with questions about the *Belgrano* which was not to provide any more information.

During the winding-up speech in the Debate John Stanley tried to assert that certain highly classified submarine operations might be compromised by Dalyell's line of questioning. This was a new argument only put forward three years after the event and if it is so convincing one can only wonder why it was not used before. Also it is difficult to see why submarine operations should require the cover up of the real nature of the change in the ROE on 2 May or the decision to attack the *25 De Mayo* on 30 April.

PART III

THE FUTURE

CHAPTER EIGHT

THE FUTURE OF OFFICIAL SECRECY

The trial was over. It had been a long, hard six months' battle by a small, but dedicated legal team fighting the massive power of the State. We had to face a vetted jury, part of the trial *in camera* and a summing up by the judge that left us with no legal defence. Yet despite all of this I was acquitted, probably because the jury did not like the way in which the judge had interpreted 'the interests of the State' as being the same as 'the political interests of the Government'. This was widely seen as victory for commonsense and a blow for democracy by the jury. Whatever the reasons it was a great relief for me and Sally and a tremendous triumph for my legal team.

After the verdict there was, not unexpectedly, a major political row involving all the party leaders. The debate concentrated on why I had been prosecuted, the future of the Official Secrets Act and why the *Belgrano* had been sunk. The implications of the result and any political capital that might be made from it were issues that no longer affected us. My own future in the Civil Service was obviously at an end and a few days after the trial I submitted my resignation.

Had it all been worth it? The whole issue could have been resolved if I had been allowed to resign in August 1984, or if I had been dismissed. Once the decision to prosecute had been taken I was determined to fight. The fight was exhausting but ultimately worthwhile. What I disliked most was being thrown into the centre of a major political controversy and being the subject of media attention. This book has been written simply to set down the story as I saw it from the inside and how these events impinged on some of the major issues that are still the subject of political debate.

But what of the events that sparked off this whole episode? Why was the *General Belgrano* sunk and why was there a cover up? The military case for sinking the *General Belgrano* as it appeared to the War Cabinet at lunchtime on 2 May 1982 was strong. It would have been difficult for any Government to reject the clear advice of the Chief of the Defence Staff that he needed action to counter what he believed was a major Argentinian attack. Whether there was *in fact* such an attack underway is another matter. What is also clear is that when the *General Belgrano* was finally sunk about eight hours later the picture had changed. The immediate threat had been replaced by a ship outside the Exclusion Zone, probably over 200 miles from the Task Force, and even worse it had been sailing away for almost half a day. This was a more difficult decision to defend in public, but not impossible if a courageous stand had been taken that the *General Belgrano* was simply a threat whatever the exact sequence of events. The position though was complicated by a lack of a clear public warning to the Argentinians covering these circumstances, and there were doubts inside the Government about the adequacy of the 23 April warning. The sinking did not sit easily with the Government's overall position that all UK military action was in strict self-defence.

Information about what had really taken place on 2 May may have been patchy in London when John Nott made his statement two days later. The statement contained a number of inaccuracies but also sought to convey the impression that the *General Belgrano* had been an immediate threat and that the Task Force had acted in self-defence. Once this account had been adopted the Government decided to stick to it and only make changes under the most extensive pressure. Why they did this is not clear. The only result was that the issue became a long running battle assuming greater and greater importance. As the battle raged so various different theories emerged, some based on evidence some not. Over the two years from May 1982 a number of wrong and misleading statements were made to Parliament. They remained uncorrected. As the inconsistencies in the Government's explanations mounted so suspicions grew about what might have happened.

By the end of 1984 virtually everything about the Government's original explanation of the sinking had been shown to be inaccurate. That it had taken so long to arrive at a roughly truthful account of events says much about the obsession with secrecy and the unwillingness of the Government to admit that it might have been wrong. At the end of all of this activity what are the questions that still remain to be answered about the sinking of the *General Belgrano*?

1. If the *General Belgrano* was a threat why was it not attacked on 1 May when it was steaming towards the Task Force which was under Argentinian air attack?
2. If the *General Belgrano* was a threat why was the information about its sighting on the afternoon of 1 May not passed on outside Northwood until late morning on 2 May?
3. What was the real relationship between Ministers and their military advisers? How much information did Ministers have about operations and how much political control was actually exercised?
4. Just what happened in Washington, Lima and London on 1/2 May? Did the War Cabinet really know nothing about the Peruvian peace plan until three hours after the sinking?

Despite all the attempts to dampen down the controversy questions remain and it is unlikely that the *General Belgrano* will be allowed to rest quietly at the bottom of the South Atlantic.

The sinking of this elderly Argentinian cruiser was the issue over which this particular battle for 'The Right to Know' took place. But the other fundamental issues remain – the future of Section 2, Freedom of Information and the level of Whitehall secrecy.

The Official Secrets Act and the question of Freedom of

Information are back on the political agenda. Lord Scarman, one of the most senior Law Lords, has called for the repeal of Section 2 of the Official Secrets Act 'lock, stock and barrel'. All three Opposition parties are in favour of Freedom of Information legislation. But the Government has used the sweeping and draconian powers in Section 2 with renewed vigour. My own trial showed just how wide those powers are and how they can be used to prosecute those who do not damage national security but merely tell Parliament how they are being misled by the Government. Although the Government shows no signs of willingness to respond to the calls for greater Freedom of Information the pressures will not be dissipated simply by inaction. How might the campaign develop over the next few years and what will be the main issues?

If the level of official secrecy is to be pushed to the top of the political agenda we need to know why it is so important and what tangible benefits might flow from radical change. Based on my own experience in Whitehall I believe that there are two basic and linked reasons why FOI is important. First, its implementation would improve the quality of decision taking in Whitehall by improving the flow and range of information. Second, FOI is about 'The Right to Know': it is a statement about where real power in a democratic society ought to lie. We must ask ourselves whether that right should, in effect, be restricted to the upper echelons in Whitehall and the 'establishment' or whether it should be diffused much more widely in society. Why should information be restricted to what Government chooses to make available to those they govern. Surely a genuinely self-confident democracy can and should believe in a wide and well-informed public debate?

In my view claustrophobic decision taking in Whitehall will continue to produce disastrous results simply because it precludes genuine open debate, and as a consequence powerful vested interests with access to the levers of power in Whitehall can exercise undue influence at the expense of the broader aspects of the public interest. While the decision taking process remains deliberately shrouded in mystery the vital process of learning from past mistakes does not take place.

Government secrecy also affects the individual because poor decision taking is not the only price we pay. Inefficiency and waste can be covered up. Information about such practices can be restricted to those circles which will be less inclined to demand exposure and radical reform.

I feel sure that those who dismiss the long struggle for the real facts of the *'Belgrano* Affair' as a 'bore' would feel very differently if the same cavalier approach to their 'Right to Know' was being applied to vital issues of direct importance to them and their children.

If people were better informed and so more able to influence the decision taking process then this would bring about a major change in the way in which British democracy works. To Whitehall this is not an attractive proposition. Information is power. Take away the exclusive right of Whitehall to control information and its power is reduced and that of the ordinary individual increased. Top civil servants tend naturally to subscribe to the view that closed government is rational government. My own experience inside Whitehall suggests the opposite. Closed government puts too much power in the hands of the Civil Service. It does not lead to cool rational decision taking in the interests of the community as a whole. It leads instead to ill-thought out decisions based only on the information which is internally available. Arguments are not pushed through to their logical conclusion and too often the determining factor may turn out to be short-term political interests or bureaucratic inertia. The closed system also increases the power of those interest groups who have easy access to Whitehall and who can ensure that their views receive far greater weight than those groups who try to represent a wider public interest.

Closed government ensures that 'official' information is overvalued compared to information generally available. There is in my experience a dangerous tendency to over-value classified information. Superficial analyses of the political and financial prospects for some Third World country are solemnly classified 'Secret' or even 'Top Secret' and duly regarded as significant. No doubt important decisions are taken based on this information. I always thought that a much better, and more up-to-date, picture could be gained by reading the newspapers.

Will Whitehall reform itself and give up its control over information voluntarily? The experience of the 'Croham Directive' in the late 1970s gives the clear answer 'no'. Its aims have never been fulfilled. Background papers have been made available only as additional public relations material. Closed government devalues the contributions of 'outsiders' in the decision taking process. I was able to observe a clear case of this at work inside MOD. Considerable 'unofficial' help was given to a number of the outside institutes that specialise in studying strategic and defence problems such as the International Institute of Strategic Studies, Chatham House or the much less prestigious Royal United Services Institute. They produced a number of studies on various strategic problems but all based on publicly available information. The published studies were usually greeted with amused contempt within MOD. They were 'useful' if they took the existing departmental line but they were never taken into account during the decision taking process. Occasionally the idea would be floated that MOD should commission a study from one of the outside bodies. This was usually dismissed because they did not know enough to join in the 'advanced' level of debate inside the Ministry. Why did they not know enough? Because MOD would not release any additional information. Why not? Because it was 'classified'. The only result of this policy was that debate about policy options was restricted to the vested interest groups inside MOD (the three Services in particular) and no alternatives were put forward. The outside bodies become frustrated because they are ignored and ignored because they are frustrated. I have no doubt similar stories could be told in other areas of Whitehall.

This brings me back to the second crucial aspect of

Freedom of Information – the proposal is not just an academic proposition to improve the flow of information. It is a fundamental statement about the way in which decisions should be taken in a democracy and who should have enough information to be involved in the debate.

Naturally Governments find life easier if they are able to debate policy questions in private, listen to those interest groups they find congenial or which are very powerful and then take decisions that maximise their own political advantage. But is this the best way of taking decisions from the point of view of the governed? The answer has to be 'No'. In a democracy ordinary citizens should have the right to participate in the decisions that affect their ordinary everyday life.

Freedom of Information would open up the decision taking process. It would enable ordinary people and small, often local, pressure groups to obtain access to important information affecting their own futures. With this information they will be able to challenge and question the decisions that are being taken elsewhere inside the bureaucracy whether in Whitehall or closer to home in the town halls. Genuine democracy is not a matter of simply voting once every four of five years for an MP and local councillor and then allowing the elected politicians a relatively free hand, in conjunction with the bureaucracy and important vested interests, to take whatever decisions they think best or most politically advantageous. Genuine democracy is about participation in decision taking. It involves a whole public debate about policy before decisions are taken and not afterwards.

Freedom of Information cannot be achieved whilst Section 2 of the Official Secrets Act remains on the statute book. Repeal of Section 2 will not, in itself, achieve Freedom of Information, but what it will do is remove one of the most universally condemned and anachronistic pieces of legislation from the statute book.

My trial at the Old Bailey clearly demonstrated both its fundamental weaknesses and its arbitrary nature. One of the basic principles of the criminal law is that there must be certainty of application. In other words a person must know what actions involve breaking the law and therefore the risk of prosecution. The Official Secrets Act is breached literally thousands of times every day. This is inevitable as it covers every single piece of official information. We have ended up with an arbitrary system that selects certain offences as meriting prosecution. The power to operate this arbitrary system of selection is in the hands of a Government Minister – the Attorney-General. He is supposed to act only as the guardian of the 'national interest' in agreeing to prosecutions. But this is a superhuman task for any politician. It will be difficult for any Attorney-General to separate the interests of his own party and Government from the wide 'national interest' and all too easy to equate the two. The present Attorney-General has not explained publicly, or to the Commons, how he decided on the 'public interest' in exercising his discretion in my case or how it will operate in future.

My trial has also highlighted the Act's weaknesses. The offence was passing two pieces of paper to an unauthorised person, albeit a duly elected Member of Parliament. The prosecution described the disclosure as 'a breach of confidence' and accepted that disclosure did not damage national security. Nevertheless the Official Secrets Act was rolled out leading to a gruelling eleven-day trial at the Old Bailey which cost the public about £75,000. I fully accept the need for disciplinary measures to deal with breaches of trust. What I do not accept is that when only the reputation and integrity of the Government has been called into question it should have available legislation to turn people into criminals.

Nobody had ever been prosecuted before for passing information to a Member of Parliament. Indeed only a few years before the Government had firmly indicated that no prosecution would be brought in such circumstances. While the Official Secrets Act remains on the statute book any Government can decide to prosecute any technical breach of the Act in an entirely arbitrary way whenever it chooses.

The case has brought out vital and worrying aspects of Section 2, in particular the way in which the judge, Mr Justice McCowan, interpreted the law. First, he ruled that Section 2 did not require the accused to have a 'guilty mind' (*mens rea*) when the offence was committed. It was in other words an 'absolute offence' whereby the simple passing of documents constituted an offence even though the accused might think, as I had done, that I was acting 'in the interests of the State' at the time I posted the documents to Tam Dalyell. This goes against virtually the whole of the rest of the criminal law where *mens rea* is a vital ingredient of any offence. It was also contrary to the ruling in the Jonathan Aitken case in 1971 where both the prosecution and the judge accepted that *mens rea* was an ingredient of a Section 2 offence.

Second, and most important, Mr Justice McCowan made a ruling about what constituted the 'interests of the State' which could have fundamental long-term consequences. The exact phrase in Section 2 is 'Duty to communicate in the interests of the State'. McCowan interpreted 'duty' as meaning only 'official duty'. This very restrictive ruling means that a civil servant could legally only ever pass information if it was his official duty to do so. Taken by itself this would effectively remove the scope for any unauthorised disclosure or any moral or civic duty to act in the public interest. The most crucial interpretation made by McCowan was that 'the interests of the State' was to be read as the policies of the organs of government as they are and not as they ought to be. He then excluded Parliament from the organs of government and went on to say that 'the interests of the State' was synonymous with the political interests of the Government of the day.

The implications of this interpretation are staggering. In law it means that under Section 2 the only way of legally passing information is if it is 'authorised' or part of 'official duty' – in other words only if it is in the interests of Ministers. There is no escape clause allowing 'unauthorised' communication in the wider public interest. In an ideal world this might be acceptable on the assumption that this and any future Government would always act with impeccable standards and absolute integrity and always put the public interest above all else. But what happens, if in the real world, the Government should happen to act, or be tempted to act, illegally or corruptly? A civil servant who knew what was happening would have no moral duty and no legal means of communicating information about these activities even to a Member of Parliament! As many commentators recognised this is the start of the road to authoritarianism and eventually tyranny. The identification of the Government with the 'state' is usually only found in extreme regimes whether of the 'left' or the 'right'. It is alien to any democratic system where the balance of power between the different elements of the state – Government, Parliament and the judiciary, is crucial to securing continuing freedom and ensuring that no one element predominates. For an English judge to exclude Parliament from the 'organs of government' is almost incredible and goes against all the fundamentals of the British constitution and the clear and unambiguous rule that Ministers retain office as long as they can command the confidence of a majority in the House of Commons. Although the jury in my case rejected the judge's ruling on the law it still remains as a ruling of a High Court judge. Moreover, the next day the Attorney-General, Sir Michael Havers, told MPs that he entirely agreed with the interpretation of the law given by the judge. I find it hard to believe that Sir Michael Havers would take the same view if he were in Opposition. As *The Times* in its major leader on 25 February said:

> Even as a legal direction concerned with the narrow point at issue in the trial it was a disgraceful statement. That the Attorney-General should endorse it as he did was both disgraceful and damaging. Is there nobody on the Treasury bench who is capable of seeing how damaging, inept and fundamentally ill-conceived is Mr Justice McCowan's direction as a standard text to define

the intricacies of the British constitution... Ministers should attempt to... remind the public that it is our multi-party system, not the policies of the day, which deserve the highest protection. That is indeed the national interest.

This raises the question of whether, if Section 2 is going to be applied in this way, it should be allowed to stay on the statute book in a democratic country. In the past one of the assumptions made by the opponents of reform has been that although Section 2 may be unsatisfactory it could stay on the statute book because no Government would really use its admittedly draconian powers to their full extent. The present Government has revitalised Section 2 and shown that it is prepared to use it in a variety of cases and in circumstances where national security has not been endangered. In my trial the law was interpreted in a way that surely cannot be accepted in a truly democratic society.

The most important reform of Section 2 is therefore to reduce its scope drastically. It is absurd to protect by means of the criminal law and up to two years' imprisonment even unclassified official information. Clearly information that would seriously damage national security, foreign policy or financial and economic interests needs to be protected. The Franks Committee back in 1972 struck the right balance in suggesting that information graded 'SECRET' and above, and some other sensitive information, should be protected by the criminal law. For all other material the use of the normal disciplinary procedures in the Civil Service would be quite sufficient. In reforming the Act it would also be important to radically revise the current section 2 (2) of the Act which makes receipt of official information a criminal offence.

It is also essential for any new Act to provide a clear public interest defence. In my trial at the Old Bailey the defence case rested on an admittedly obscure part of the Act. We argued with imagination and hard work that Parliament had intended to leave an 'escape clause' in the Act for unauthorised communication in exceptional cases in the public interest. The judge's ruling removed this one way round the all-embracing effect of Section 2. Although I was acquitted by the jury this leaves the position muddy and only demonstrates the need for a clear public interest defence. If the Government does decide to prosecute then the defendant must have the right to use such a defence. The Government cannot be the sole judge of the 'public interest'. That should be left for the jury to decide on the facts of each case.

The need for reform of Section 2 and the implementation of Freedom of Information is urgent. In David Steel's words: 'The level of secrecy in Britain today has reached proportions that seriously undermine the health of our democracy.' In the Official Secrets Act the Government has one of the most powerful weapons ever passed by Parliament. In the past it has been used capriciously and in peculiar circumstances. It is now being used with greater determination and more frequently, not to protect national secrets but to punish those who annoy the Government or demonstrate its own deception of Parliament and the people. As Clement Freud said in 1979 it gives 'more power than a bad man should have or a good man should need'.

Freedom of Information is equally important if the power of the bureaucracy in Whitehall and its associated special interest groups is to be reduced and the power of ordinary citizens increased. Governments naturally want to keep power to themselves. But in a mature democracy the people are involved in decisions that affect their lives, their future and the future of their children. They have a right to know.

If my own prosecution and trial contribute in some way to the repeal of Section 2 of the Official Secrets Act and the eventual passage of a genuine Freedom of Information Act then the experience will have been worthwhile.